The Complete Book of Sisters

in the same series

THE COMPLETE BOOK OF AUNTS
THE COMPLETE BOOK OF MOTHERS-IN-LAW

The Complete Book of Sisters

LUISA DILLNER

ILLUSTRATED BY STEPHANIE VON REISWITZ

faber and faber

First published in 2009
by Faber and Faber Limited
Bloomsbury House
74–77 Great Russell Street
London WC1B 3DA

Typeset by Faber and Faber Limited
Printed in the UK by CPI Mackays, Chatham

A CIP record for this book
is available from the British Library

ISBN 978–0–571–24800–1

2 4 6 8 10 9 7 5 3 1

To my brother Larry and Esther and Tivka (his daughters),
and to Madeleine, Mathilda and Lydia (who are mine)

Contents

Me and My Brother 1

1 The Psychology of Sisters 9

2 A History of Sisters 21

3 Sisters as Rivals 51

4 Elder and Younger Sisters 73

5 Beloved Sisters 93

·6 Campaigning Sisters 123

7 Sisters of Powerful Men 137

8 Multiple Sisters 153

9 Brothers and Sisters 173

10 Fairy-tale Sisters 199

11 Celebrity Sisters 205

12 Royal Sisters 225

13 Criminal Sisters 241

14 A Wider Family of Sisters 255

15 How to Be a Good Sister 269

Acknowledgements 275

Me and My Brother

I don't have a sister but I am one, and when I was six I prayed for two things: a Sindy doll and for my brother to disappear. A sister who is four years younger than her brother is of no use to a boy, so mostly we fought. We were so good at fighting that my mother never wanted to leave us alone together. On the rare occasion she risked it she would return to scenes of carnage and accusations that took hours to for her to adjudicate. Hence my feeling that I would be better off without him.

Our parents called us Luisa and Larry but it could have been worse as our father had considered Arvid and Astrid. My brother didn't take too well to my arrival and I enjoyed hearing of his distress on finding me at home on his return from nursery school.

At school I was the good girl but he was the memorable boy – he had a reputation for being funny and politically opinionated. He was so opinionated that he was excluded from school for one day for making a stand. People's faces would light up when he came into the room because he could tell a good story and make people laugh; he was socially able while I was shy. Late into my teens anyone who knew the both of us would ask, 'Where's Larry?' as though I on my own was not enough. At parents' evening my glowing report would be dismissed in five minutes by the teachers who were more interested in telling my parents about my brother's poor academic results.

We didn't share confidences. It was an unpromising beginning. I'm not sure how I missed it, but I didn't realise when he
and my father started arguing furiously, about anything. My
father's own upbringing as the child of divorced, impoverished
parents in Chicago had made him ill equipped to bring up a
teenage son. They fought over everything, even how much butter my brother was putting on his bread. To my shame, when
my teenage brother stopped being at home, I didn't think
much of it and I don't remember missing him. I went to see him
in London with my mother once, to a squat he was sharing in
Mornington Crescent, and he made out he was fine, although
the squat seemed anything but fine to me.

He could have continued being distant but he changed
everything. I don't know why or if it was even intentional but
two moments defined the shift in our relationship. The first
was when we were sitting in a coffee shop the summer
before I was going to university and he
tried to talk to me about sex and
relationships, perhaps worry-
ing with some justification
that I was a late developer.
It was an adult conversa-
tion, my first with him,
and I remember being
incredulous that he was
talking to me like a real
person. The next event
was when he spontaneously
gave me £200 to go travelling after my first year at uni-

versity. I used it to pay for a flight to America. It was extraordinarily generous, especially since he himself had never flown.

I would be surprised now if our relationship is so very different from that of two sisters who are close. We can't share make-up (neither of us has any) or the common understanding of being the same sex but we speak often on the phone, and if we are miserable we tell each other. We share triumphs, trivial frustrations and our history, which as we grow older has had desperately sad moments. Sarah, his wife, died of breast cancer when she was thirty-nine and it was heartbreaking. I remember the first time I met her, at a Belgian restaurant, and he was so excited because she was lovely, smart and funny, and inside I was thinking, 'I'm not sure if you'll impress me.' But she did impress me because she was a gorgeous woman who loved life. When she was ill I used to speak to her on the phone about Larry and promise to watch out for him and Esther, their daughter, neither of which I've done very well. It took a long while for Larry to recover; he has a partner and four more children and they have made him enjoy life again. Sarah's death made me feel overwhelming emotion for him; I would have done a lot to have taken some of his pain away.

I'm sure I annoy him but he is patient, even when I have strident views about which school a child of his should go to. If I was him I would tell me to shut up. If he wants to be open he will be but I sometimes have to interrogate him to find out how he feels. He is more comfortable telling funny stories sometimes.

I never think of him not being there. We tease each other about whom our mother loves the most and whom she'll leave her grand piano to (which we will take as proof of who was her favourite). I'll be fine if he gets it.

My brother on me

One version of the story sees sixteen-year-old brother chasing twelve-year-old sister around a tennis court, racket raised, because she's constantly messing about. The other has sister chasing brother around aforementioned court because he's taking the game too seriously. Luisa and I have been rewriting this particular piece of our history virtually since it happened. And in fairness, at the time, she had good cause to be threatening (I can't believe I'm still perpetuating this).

I'd had, though, four years to give the teachers at my grammar school sufficient reason to form an association between the name Dillner and (lack of) academic interest, and I was conscious when my sister joined the school that it wasn't going to be in her favour. Judging by how well she got on, I guess she must have told the teachers that I was actually her foster brother and they believed her.

I chose to go straight into publishing and journalism, and while starting your own regional business magazine company creates a kind of nodding approval among family and friends, it doesn't really compare to sister going to university and qualifying as a doctor.

Then, having gained the mantle for sibling status, she successfully applies for a post with the *British Medical Journal* – demonstrating that the mantle is still going to be hers even when she decides to venture into my line of work.

I broadened my repertoire to edit a couple of books and pen the occasional column in obscure trade journals (I can't even remember their names) – she wrote a couple of books which merited radio and television interviews and has been a columnist in the national press such as the *Guardian*.

Just recounting the highlights (and I suppose that depends on whose perspective you're coming from here) should be enough to make me despair, although, and you knew this irony was coming, my sister is the one person I'd turn to if that happened.

It won't, because I've always been proud of her. I was going to add the words 'for some reason', but actually I know exactly why. It goes back to the days when she took a Saturday job at the weekly newspaper I was publishing. Not only was she intuitively empathic with the locals, an impressive characteristic for a teenager, but her writing found the heart and soul of the story (or touched the nerve if need be). And this wasn't some upstart – it was my sister.

I guess I see myself in her strengths and weaknesses (albeit in different measures). That's a different basis from the relationship you have with a best friend. The blood tie provides what in my commercial writing I'd describe as unique value added.

I'm sure that kinship was a contributory factor in her being able to help me recalibrate after my wife died. It wasn't anything to do with whether she knew the right things to say but that I was able to talk to her about anything and everything, the realisation (now) that obviously I had implicit trust, I could say anything to her without attempting to hide or shade emotion.

I know from asking people who know us both that Luisa and I share a slightly belligerent streak (it's genetic of course), which happily means that we tend not to take offence at what the other is saying. Another symptom is that telephone calls with Luisa (and probably me in that case) usually have a peremptory conclusion, with the sound of the dialling tone rather than a goodbye sometimes.

If I had more than one sister or a brother even, would that sense of kinship with Luisa be any less, or would I just get more of it because of the others? The answer is, of course, I don't know. It'll be something our respective sons and daughters can experience though. We both went for big families.

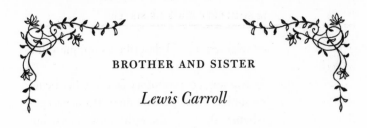

BROTHER AND SISTER

Lewis Carroll

'SISTER, sister, go to bed!
Go and rest your weary head.'
Thus the prudent brother said.

'Do you want a battered hide,
Or scratches to your face applied?'
Thus his sister calm replied.

'Sister, do not raise my wrath.
I'd make you into mutton broth
As easily as kill a moth.'

The sister raised her beaming eye
And looked on him indignantly
And sternly answered, 'Only try!'

Off to the cook he quickly ran.
'Dear Cook, please lend a frying-pan
To me as quickly as you can.'

'And wherefore should I lend it you?'
'The reason, Cook, is plain to view.
I wish to make an Irish stew.'

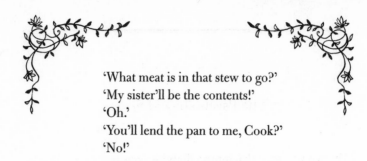

'What meat is in that stew to go?'
'My sister'll be the contents!'
'Oh.'
'You'll lend the pan to me, Cook?'
'No!'

Moral: Never stew your sister.

1

The Psychology of Sisters

My two youngest daughters climb into our bed on a Saturday morning; still young enough to have that sleepy child smell and warm tousled hair. It will be cuddles and laughter for all of five minutes. And then it will start. One of them will have stolen the favourite spot in the bed to the right of me, the other will feel short-changed on the cuddles, and so they will start prodding each other with their little fingers, then kicking, until there is a crescendo of shrieks and bodies furiously hurling themselves at each other. Then they will stomp off downstairs where we will find them, arms wrapped round each other affectionately and calmly on the sofa. This is the essence of sisterhood. Few people can make you as angry as a sister can (from an early age), or make you feel as safe and loved. I see it in my three girls and I wish I could stop the rivalry so that their relationship would be all sweetness and light. I try to do all the things the experts tell you to do, not to label or compare and to reassure them there's enough love to go round. Only my eldest daughter, ten years older than the youngest, graciously understands this.

But all the sisters I have talked to for this book, however different their relationships, have uttered universal truths about sisterhood. No sisterly relationship is the same; there is not even a typical one. But this jostling for position, some separating through rivalry is probably inevitable, as is the feeling that a sister is a mixed blessing. Sisters may be uniquely placed both to love and to hate each other. This is a lifelong relationship that shares and reinforces childhood memories. In her book, *Original Kin: The Search for Connection among Adult Sisters and Brothers*, Marian Sandmaier says that even when our parents die, our siblings keep them alive for us through shared memories, such that 'we are never entirely orphaned'.

This book is about all sisters, so it includes sisters who have brothers as well. The relationship between brother and sister is different because they are not the same sex and so not as easy to benchmark or rail against. But elder sisters spoke of feeling diminished by a younger brother who was brighter or more physically able and sporty. Elder brothers told of being irritated by younger sisters who seemed to get all the affection and less of the discipline. I remember my son cutting off my oldest daughter's curls because 'she wanted a haircut'. He wanted, I believe, not only to get my attention but to make her look less cute.

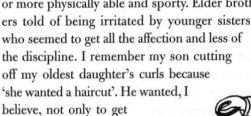

The sibling conflicts of childhood do not set the tone for the relationship thereafter, because your relationship with a sister is a fluid and changing one, but there may be early interactions that do become hardwired. Judy Dunn's influential study of forty families in the Cambridge area, *Siblings: Love, Envy and Understanding*, starting just before the birth of a second child and lasting for twelve months overall, found that although almost all the elder siblings were affected by the new arrival, the majority were affectionate and concerned about the baby. Dunn found a link between how much a mother talked to her child (most were between one and a half and two years old) about the baby and how often the child wanted to help or cuddle the baby. Other studies that have looked at how six-year-old children relate to their siblings suggest that patterns of behaviour early on hold true for years afterwards. So the six-year-olds who were fond of their siblings had shown affection to them within the first few months of their birth. Dunn found that at an early age children could feel empathy and concern for their sisters and brothers. She found that the relationship between siblings was characterised by all of the following: pleasure, affection, hostility, aggression, jealousy, rivalry and frustration.

Young children have a great capacity for telling tales on each other as well as fighting and paradoxically sticking up for each other in the face of a parental telling-off. They may be delighted when they can frame their sister for a naughtiness they did themselves, but many sisters I spoke to remembered with ludicrous amounts of guilt the occasions on which they had done so.

It isn't clear what parents need to do to foster the positive elements of sibling interactions but there's some evidence for what they shouldn't do. Much damage has been done to the relationship between sisters who have variously been labelled as the pretty, smart, or conversely the not so smart one, by careless or even well-meaning parents. It is natural to compare children but dreadfully unhelpful to them. Where a child comes in the birth order may make labels even more troublesome; the oldest one has to be responsible, the middle child may have to negotiate between an elder and younger sister, and the youngest may forever be the baby of the family. Psychologists refer to the tyranny of having a younger sister, whose wishes (and curls) dominate the family. A childhood friend of mine had two sisters and a mother who openly discussed the attributes of each child while doing the school run. The oldest one was the intelligent one who was going to medical school, the middle one (my friend) was quite, but not *that* smart, and the youngest was the pretty one. I wonder if my friend, who has a job in the leisure industry, wanted to do something more academic but felt she would have disappointed her mother.

The childhood of sisters is full of comparisons from the external world as well as from within the family. A teacher at my children's primary school who had taught my son (the oldest child) slipped into another class to watch how his sister behaved, to see if his inability to concentrate ran through his siblings. Other teachers have asked if one of the girls is better than the other at music and friends have commented on how pretty one of them is in front of another. A belated 'You're pretty too' doesn't wash even with young children. So sisters frankly get their noses rubbed in their differences. Left to themselves they would have noticed who was the taller, the one with the conventionally pretty nose, the one who can sing. They would have decided how to rationalise their differences and felt some of the unavoidable sibling rivalry that comes from having a sister. I hope they still will. Other girls at school may be prettier and smarter than you but they don't, like your sister, live at your house.

Sometimes this competition extends to who has the most parental love. Children struggle with the concept of infinite love; whatever is handed to their sister diminishes them. Parents may be anxious to eliminate rivalry but they can't. They can try to be fair, to not hold one sister up as a model for the other and to be careful to keep their secrets confidential. If they insist on sisters being best friends it is just as likely to make them enemies.

By the time sisters reach adolescence the competition of childhood may give way to a different sort of relationship. A younger sister may look at her elder one with envy but also admiration. Elder sisters are enormously influential, glamorous and mysterious. A younger sister can watch from a safe distance as her sister becomes a sexual being, struggles for independence from their parents and chooses a career. This can be a turning point: the separation that makes it possible for sisters to become closer. Only when you separate from a sister can you feel you are her equal.

In her book *Sistering: Power and Change in Female Relationships*, Melanie L. Mauthner defines distinct types of sister relationships: best friends, close companionship and distant companionship. She found that sisters who described themselves as best friends socialised together, said they each knew what the other was thinking and would tease each other. They also corroborated or gently disagreed with family stories. These relationships were confiding and intimate. The intensity of the friendship did not rely on how often they saw each other but on how much they understood each other.

The close companionate relationships were less intense but still had close bonds and the more distant ones had a lower level of contact and less emotional involvement. In the more distant relationships sisters would say that they couldn't always trust each other, that there was a lot of envy in their relationship. More than one of the women I spoke to said that they were estranged from a sister, relating it to an incident in their sister's life such as a psychological breakdown. Even in distant relationships women talk about their sisters as if they really want to talk about them. They usually spoke with compassion and understanding of them, however poor their relationship was, and although often resigned to their estrangement, they were wistful about their sisters in a way that suggested they wished it was different.

Distant relationships belie the clichés about sisters; that they are always there for you and that blood is thicker than water. But they may be the result of other clichés about sisters; that no one can hurt or betray you like a sister.

This is the darker side to sisterhood that is not all about closeness and support. Sisters can disappoint each other, they can steal boyfriends and reduce achievements by being more successful. They can know how best to upset a sister, the childhood memories that put them in a bad light; they, more than other people, may really know who their sister is.

As sisters grow older, as they marry and have children, it can become easier to be friends. Melanie Mauthner quotes a study finding that one third of married women say their sister is the person they most confide in. Generally as sisters get older they mellow and some of the tensions of their earlier relationship ease; their sister is less of a threat. I spoke to sisters who said their relationship was incredibly important because their sisters were the one constant in their lives. But that didn't mean it was always unproblematic. 'No one can hurt you like your sister,' said one woman. 'With a man you have more in your armoury because you can leave him, you have the nuclear option. You don't have that with a sister. On the other hand if I killed someone I know my sister would borrow a bulldozer and help me dig a hole.'

Amy Fleming on her sister

Like most siblings, my sister Sarah and I are the same, only different. She takes after our mother, responsible and good-natured with chestnut hair and eyes, whereas I'm fair, undisciplined and squally, more like our dad. Sarah, a proper beauty, is taller, slimmer-hipped and has more pronounced cheekbones than me. She arrived two years before me, so I carved out my little niche to fit around her and complement her. I generally like to play the droll little sister.

The first time we were separated was when Sarah left our home in London to attend university in Brighton. I was too preoccupied with exploring Soho's nightclubs, gaining experience of a romantic nature and deciding whether or not I should go back to school (I had left after my GCSEs) to be that bothered. Sometimes, however, I would poke around her uninhabited bedroom to see what she had left behind.

During term time, our lives became largely separate bar my occasional weekend visits to Brighton. If I was feeling sad or lost, I would want to see my sister. She's a no-nonsense person and is good at looking after me, and breaking me out of a deep funk.

When I was twenty-three, we were both living in London again. While we remained fundamentally close, we often wouldn't see each other for as long as a month or two. Sarah was going out with an Australian and his UK visa was due to expire, so she decided to go travelling before moving to Sydney for a while. This plan made perfect sense and I was happy for her. After all, long-distance telephone lines were getting better and cheaper all the time, so we would still be able to talk.

When it came to the night of her leaving party I was tired. I showed my face but when things started getting rowdy, I said my farewells and set off to catch the last tube. Very quickly, panic started rising from the pit of my stomach. I was staring into a vast, Sarah-less abyss. The street I was standing in, and the weekend cacophony, started whirling around me. I ran back to her flat, tears streaming from my eyes. I hadn't expected to feel so distraught, but I cried most of the following day too.

There's something about the sweetness of Sarah's spirit that has the capacity to make me weep intensely. If I were an actor needing to summon tears, my failsafe equivalent of imagining my dog was dead would be to recall the image of ten-year-old Sarah standing alone on our street holding two plastic bags for us to slide down a snowy hill on again. I went off to ride on Claire Anningson's fancy wooden sleigh instead and

there wasn't room for her. It doesn't matter that Sarah had been equally mean to me on many occasions (for years, that girl could make me do almost anything simply by threatening never to speak to me again). Picturing her excited face, those big, dark eyes, crumpling as she turned back towards our house still upsets me.

Sarah eventually married her Australian, in Devon, where our father lives (our parents split up when I was sixteen). The newlyweds were to stay in England for a few years before eventually settling in Australia. It was to be a small, fairly informal wedding and I was the only bridesmaid. I was thrilled for Sarah. Even so, part of me went into denial about her imminent nuptials. I left finding a dress, for example, until the last minute, and ended up choosing something deeply unflattering.

On the morning of the wedding, I fell quiet. When the flowers arrived, followed by the photographer to document Sarah's preparations, I couldn't understand how everyone was carrying on as if this were nothing out of the ordinary. Daddy showed up, every inch the dapper father-of-the-bride, and he, too, acted as though the situation were perfectly normal. As though my mother giving Sarah her antique silk dressing gown – 'something old' – with no prior word about it to me was nothing out of the ordinary.

Looking back, I now wonder whether I had been troubled by Sarah leaving our family, so publicly and officially, to start her own. And, silly as it may sound, the dressing gown, which had always hung reassuringly on my mother's bedroom door, was going off to live with this new family too.

Soon we arrived at the back of the town hall for the ceremony. When we reached the end of the aisle, I turned to face the room to read a poem. 'On Waterloo Bridge,' I began. And that was as far as I got before I let out a series of ugly, uncontrollable sobs. I'm pretty sure I managed to finish the poem, but my face twitched with suppressed anguish for the duration of the ceremony. (I managed to cheer up plenty for the reception.)

Eight years later and I have just learned that plans are afoot for Sarah, who lives around the corner from me with her husband and two young children, to relocate with her family to Australia within the next year. I'm in denial.

2

A History of Sisters

Being a sister has been recognised throughout history. A sister's role and importance, however, have changed over the centuries, especially in societies where men were once the only sex that counted. Most societies have had a word and definition for a sister. The *Oxford English Dictionary* describes it plainly as 'A female in a relationship to another person or persons having the same parents'. It notes in brackets, 'Also applied to animals'. The word *sister* comes from the Old English *sweoster* with a smattering of the Old Norse *syster*. The term can also be used for non-biological sisters, chosen by someone to be as a sister, but true sisters are distinguished by being part of a family and as such cannot be either chosen or deselected.

Sisters are mentioned in stories and plays, depicted in pictures and at the hearts of political intrigues. Sisters have the full range of attributes and characteristics just as you'd expect. Being a sister has meant different things at different times but has always had an emotional component. The history of sisters is essentially the history of women. For much of history women were thought of in relation to their men, as daughters and later wives (who required dowries).

The most famous sisters in the Bible, Leah and Rachel, are not the best poster girls for the relationship. They were, however, manipulated by their father into an unenviable position. It was the younger, more beautiful Rachel with whom Jacob fell

in love in a field of sheep and asked Laban (her father) for permission to marry. Laban agreed on the condition that Jacob
worked for him for seven years. Once these years were up there
was a wedding feast and Jacob's bride was brought to him,
veiled so heavily that it wasn't until morning when he realised
he had been tricked into marrying 'tender-eyed' Leah.

Jacob was furious but accepted Laban's excuse that 'it must
not be done so in our country to give the younger before the
firstborn'. He agreed to take Rachel as his wife as well, in
return for another seven years of work.

Jacob loved Rachel more than Leah but while Leah effort-
lessly had sons, Rachel did not. The attraction of Rachel was
balanced by the fertility of Leah. Both sisters were envious of
each other. Leah reproached Rachel for stealing her husband,
to which Rachel replied, 'Jacob is not thy husband; he is mine.
It was for my sake that he came here and served our father for
so many years.' Rachel did manage to have two sons, one of
whom was Joseph.

The story may be biblical but the rivalry between sisters
reverberates through the ages. Greek mythology was written by
men, but has many mythological sisters who have attracted the
scholarly interest of feminists. In the book *Laughing with
Medusa*, Professor Simon Goldhill writes, 'There is no metaphor
more potent in modern feminism than sisterhood.' The Fates
(or the Moirae as they were also called) were the three sisters
who controlled the destiny of every mortal from birth to death.
They were said to be unfeeling old crones who arrived shortly
after a baby's birth to determine its course in life. The Graeae
are more of the same, three old women who shared an eye and
tooth between them. But they and others like them are sisters

coincidentally, whereas in Sophocles' play *Antigone* sisterhood is the story and it is a tragic one.

Antigone starts with the words 'Ismene, sister, my own dear sister'. So far so sisterly. The play's dilemma is around their brother, who has been killed, but the law forbids his sisters to bury his body because he was a traitor to Thebes. Antigone tells her sister that she will disobey Creon the king and bury her brother even if she is punished by being stoned to death. 'I will do my part – and thine, if thou wilt not – to a brother.'

Ismene, however, is a more traditional and obedient woman of ancient Greece and pleads with her sister not to go against the state, reminding her of how terrible it has already been to watch their family being killed off and how they shall 'perish, more miserably than all the rest' if they are caught. Antigone is furious and tells her that she will hate her if she continues to disagree with her.

When their brother is buried and Antigone's crime is discovered, largely because she insists on doing it in public, Ismene begs to be allowed to die alongside her: 'Nay sister, reject me not, but let me die with thee, and duly honour the dead.' But Antigone does reject her. As she goes to her death she justifies her actions on the basis that a brother is more important than a husband or child, as the latter two are replaceable, but a brother can never be. As for sisters, she doesn't mention them at all.

Simon Goldhill says that in ancient Greece it was the relationship between brothers that counted, the one on which inheritance was based and for which loyalty was expected. 'Sister', he says, 'is not a normative term of address.'

More romantically, the Pleiades star cluster (one of the best known and most easily seen) is named after seven sisters born to Atlas and Pleione, a sea nymph. The myth says that Atlas was forced to carry the heavens on his shoulders, leaving his daughters pursued by Orion. Zeus out of pity made them into stars so they could be close to their father.

Meanwhile real-life sisterhood was not without its trials. In Roman Egypt (during the first to third centuries AD) brothers and sisters, especially among privileged classes, were encouraged to marry each other. The Ptolemies were especially interested in these marriages. Evidence from census returns (preserved on papyrus) shows that in some areas of Egypt nearly a quarter of marriages were incestuous. This practice was for keeping money in the family and making it easier to prove ancestry. A favourable horoscope of the time reads, 'If a son is born in the terms of Mercury he will be successful and have great power . . . He will be brave and tall and acquire property and moreover will be married to his own sister and will have children by her.' The practice was certainly not just occasional.

Outside of Roman Egypt, however, marrying your sister did not catch on. But that didn't stop some unhealthy sibling relationships. The emperor Gaius Caligula (born in AD 12) had three sisters, of whom Drusilla was his favourite. Throughout his brutal, erratic regime he gave the women in his family public honours that were unprecedented. This has led to speculation that he had unnaturally close relationships with his sisters. In fact Robert Graves, in his translation of Suetonius' Life of Caligula, writes, 'It was his habit to commit incest with each of his three sisters in turn and at large banquets, when his wife reclined above him, he placed them all in turn below him.

They say he ravished his sister Drusilla before he came of age
. . .' Graves says that later he took Drusilla away from her husband and treated her as his wife. When she died he was so distraught he refused to let her body be taken away and made it an
offence on pain of death to laugh, bathe or dine with one's
family during a period of public mourning. Drusilla was deified
by the Roman Senate as 'Diva Drusilla' and Caligula went on to
name his only daughter after her. Drusilla's death not only
ended any intimacy with his remaining sisters but made him so
deranged that he later denounced them for allegedly plotting
against him. This view of Caligula as an incestuous brother has
been challenged by academics as a hostile attempt to portray
him as a monster, but the charges have stuck.

After the plethora of sisters in Greek mythology and the odd
story in Roman times, the history of sisters goes rather quiet. It
wasn't until 1570 that the first use of the word 'sisterly' was
recorded. Overall the history of childhood and with it the role
of siblings has been under-investigated. There has been a
tendency to think that in the Middle Ages, because of high
mortality rates (up to half of all children never reached adult-

hood) and epic childbearing (most mothers had babies every two to three years), children were not loved as they are in modern times. The fragility of life, it is supposed, meant that siblings did not bond as they do now. Yet there is no evidence to support this and some evidence to the contrary in the sorrowful writings of bereaved parents.

The most famous sisters in Shakespeare's plays are not stalwarts of sisterly behaviour. In *King Lear* and *The Taming of the Shrew* sisters are central to the plot but in neither play is sisterhood a developed theme. Sisters are there to provide stark contrasts. In *The Taming of the Shrew*, written in the 1590s, the beautiful and obedient Bianca is the opposite of her shrewish sister Katherina. The play opens with Katherina having slapped her sister and accusing her father of favouring Bianca; 'She is your treasure, she must have a husband, I must dance bare-foot on her wedding day,' she sneers at him. But the play is more about the submission of women and their relationships with men. Their father gives Katherina in marriage to Petruchio who then tames her. Ironically Bianca then briefly becomes the 'bad sister' by eloping with a penniless tutor. There is sisterly rivalry in *King Lear* (written between 1603 and 1606), as Cordelia is her father's favourite daughter and the less loved Goneril and Regan are the sisters who propel their father to his tragic self-destruction. In the first scene Lear asks his daughters who loves him the most. When his beloved Cordelia refuses to play the game she is cast out and the kingdom divided between the two 'wicked' sisters. Goneril and Regan set up their own sibling rivalry again by competing for the same young man, Edmund, which results in Goneril poisoning Regan. Goneril later stabs herself to death, Cordelia is killed and Lear dies from grief. *King Lear* was written close to the time of Queen Elizabeth I's death, a monarch who had her own experience of sibling rivalry but managed to survive her half-sister Mary's reign (see Chapter 12).

In Salem in the USA, sisters had a hard time purely by virtue of their sibling bond. Witchcraft was assumed to be hereditary, so when men and women in Salem were accused of the practice in the seventeenth century, their siblings knew that they too would be arrested. The infamous Salem witchhunts were less about witchcraft and more about the land disputes between the Putnam and the Easty families which preceeded the trials. It is no coincidence that among the tormented girls making accusations of witchcraft were Putnams (who said they were tormented into having fits) and that it was three Easty sisters who were put on trial. Of the Easty sisters Mary and Rebecca were put to death; Sarah was not. Rebecca was the first to be hanged, at the age of seventy-one, much to the outrage of some prominent members of the community, as Rebecca was clearly a respectable Christian woman. One of the Putnam women, Ann, later apologised.

The status of sisters was for much of history linked to the economics of the family. In sixteenth- and seventeenth-century

Venice this was shown rather dramatically by the number of elder sisters incarcerated in convents (there were said to be more women in convents than outside them). The cause was the price of dowries, which had become so high that families could only afford to pay one and that was usually for the youngest, so that money remained in the family for as long as possible. This was not only bitterly unjust but did nothing for the ties of sisterhood.

The need to be the most desirable sister for marriage did create some resentments and jealousies. A training manual for parents published in 1798, called *The Female Aegis*, told girls they should be kind and warned mothers not to encourage rivalry as children would be taught 'envy and malevolence'.

Gradually history reveals more than the occasional sisterly relationship. There are many examples of sisters mourning and being mourned but by the eighteenth century there is evidence of their having more modern relationships with their siblings while still alive. There are many letters from and to sisters. It was sisters who left the family home to marry and who were left behind when their brothers went off to war. Sisters who remained unwed at home were called upon by other family members to come and help out with their households and children. These absences led to letters being written. In the mid-1700s two English sisters, Barbara Postlethwaite, who left home to marry at nineteen, and her younger, unmarried sister Elizabeth, wrote numerous letters that show how sisters could be warm and intimate with each other, even when separated, as these sisters were for nearly two decades. The sisters write about vexatious maids, latest fashions in cloaks and Elizabeth's constant ill health (although she outlived her sister by over thirty years). Living apart made them anxious about each other. Elizabeth wrote to Barbara when she heard her elder sister was ill, in quite bossy terms; 'It concern [*sic*] me very much that you continue to be so low and poorly. I am afraid you have not made that drink of Mrs Townshend's, I wonder you should not, I think it's quite necessary for you.'

Sibling relationships were now more meaningful, becoming as important as those between children and parents. It became part of family life to be emotionally close to your sister. An example is the relationship between Harriet Spencer and her sister Georgiana, who became Duchess of Devonshire (and who was a famous beauty, socialite and campaigner for the Whigs), in the eighteenth century. The sisters were partners in crime against social conventions. Born into one of the wealthiest families in England, Georgiana was the glamorous older sister, Harriet the scrawny, shy one. Yet there seems to have been no sibling rivalry. Georgiana acquired a reputation for having affairs, gambling, overspending and having illegitimate children, all activities that her younger sister adopted. Neither had a happy marriage. When Georgiana became pregnant from a love affair and her husband demanded she have the baby in France it was Harriet who assumed the role of protector, accompanying her sister even though she was scared of travelling. It was she who saw her through the trauma of leaving her baby for adoption. Georgiana tried to return the favour, secretly paying off some of Harriet's gambling debts. When Georgiana died from liver disease, Harriet was holding her in her arms. She wrote afterwards: 'I saw it all, held her through all her struggles, saw her expire . . . and yet I am alive.' When Harriet did die, her coffin was placed in the family vault beside that of her beloved sister.

Sisters also became more valued by their brothers, no longer just treasured for the advantageous marriages they could make but also for their emotional support. The psychological importance of sisters, as opposed to the economic, became prominent. Some creative geniuses such as Wordsworth (see Chapter 9) relied heavily on their sisters for inspiration.

During the nineteenth century various wars saw brothers writing to sisters with deep affection, sometimes desperate for news from home. Lieutenant Jasper Hall wrote to his sister Jane in the Crimean War, imploring her to keep in touch with Carry, his intended wife, whose parents forbade him to write to her. 'I heard from Carry by the last mail, she is quite well and says you never write to her now and she thinks you have forgotten her existence. I beg that you will also write to me again soon with all news of home for I have been a long time without any.'

There are letters from General Ulysses S. Grant to his sisters from the American Civil War, in which he confided how heavily he felt the responsibilities of his role. In a letter to his sister Mary he wrote, 'For a conscientious person and I profess to be one, this is a most slavish life. I may be envied by ambitious persons, but I in turn envy the person who can transact his daily business and retire to a quiet home without a feeling of responsibility for the morrow.'

Similarly in the nineteenth century Benjamin Disraeli wrote confiding letters to his sister (who died before he became prime minister) which often sound big-headed – but, in fairness, his sister already thought he was marvellous. In 1841 he wrote to her, 'I spoke with great effect in the House, the best speech on our side; it even drew "iron tears down Pluto's cheek", alias, applause and words of praise from Peel.' Undoubtedly no one would have been more proud than his sister. When she died, Benjamin wrote to his brother Ralph; 'She was the harbour or refuge in all the storms of my life & I hoped she would have closed my eyes.'

Some sisters did not have the opportunity to be close to their siblings. The slave trade separated many siblings, often for ever. In her moving account of being sold as a slave Mary Prince, of West Indian origin, wrote in her deposition to the English parliament in 1829:

Oh dear! I cannot bear to think of that day, – it is too much. – It recalls the great grief that filled my heart, and the woeful thoughts that passed to and fro through my mind, whilst listening to the pitiful words of my poor mother, weeping for the loss of her children . . . I, as the eldest stood first, Hannah next to me, then Dinah; and our mother stood beside, crying over us . . . I then saw my sisters led forth, and sold to different owners; so that we had not the sad satisfaction of being partners in bondage . . . This is slavery.

Of course, this wasn't the only example of sisters being separated. Between 1869 and 1969 Aboriginal children were forcibly removed from their parents by the government and Church missions, with the aim of making them more 'Australian'. A report that shocked Australia, 'Bringing Them Home' by the Human Rights and Equal Opportunity Commission, estimated that between one in three and one in ten children were 'stolen' from their parents between 1910 and 1970 alone. Some sisters were never reunited with their siblings.

During the late eighteenth and nineteenth centuries sisterhood took off. There are famous novels full of sisters. *Middlemarch*, *Pride and Prejudice*, *Wives and Daughters*, *The Woman in White* and *Little Dorrit* are some of the best novels of their time. Academics have said this prevalence of sisters and feminine emotions in novels shows the emergence of women's qualities as heroic. These novels certainly illustrate the complexity of sisterly relationships and their potential for lifelong companionship. There is not enough space to pick out detail from all of these novels but sisters in each are often used as contrasts to each other. In *Pride and Prejudice* the five sisters are all 'out' at once and competing for husbands. Each is drawn distinctly so that the eldest, Jane, is beautiful and quiet, Elizabeth is smart, Lydia is thoughtless, Kitty is silly and poor Mary represents the girl so often lost in a gaggle of sisters, being plain and dull. *Middlemarch* has two very different sisters in Dorothea who is complex and Celia who is frivolous, yet as the novel progresses it is Celia who understands how life works and manipulates her husband and indeed her sister to conform in society. Dorothea has lofty ideas but the sisters are not as dissimilar as she might like to think. George Eliot was not close to her own sister, which may explain some of the distance between Dorothea and Celia.

In the hundreds of paintings of sisters that were produced at the same time there is a predominance of mythological depictions, the Three Graces and the Fates being popular. *The Ladies Waldegrave*, by Joshua Reynolds, is actually modelled on the Fates, with one sister spinning the thread of life while the other two measure and then cut it. In the 1840s there was a series of paintings that were all called *The Sisters*, by various artists, with various siblings reclining, embracing and sketching. Then the themes became more interesting, with paintings showing jealousy between sisters. In *Showing a Preference* by John Callcott Horsley, one sister sits near the piano with her admirer draped over her, while her sister looks crossly at her. Another theme in paintings of this time was the saving of a fallen woman by her virtuous sister. These paintings, it should be noted, are by men. But Christina Rossetti's poem 'Goblin Market' has a similar theme. Her brother illustrated the poem with a picture of the two sisters, Laura and Lizzie, embracing in sleep. In the poem Laura eats goblin fruit

and Lizzie saves her from death by risking an assault from the goblins to save her. In a verse that has been pored over for its sexual references (lesbianism has been suggested and you can see why, as well as temptation and redemption), Lizzie runs home to Laura and says:

> 'Eat me, drink me, love me:
> Laura, make much of me:
> For your sake I have braved the glen
> And had to do with goblin merchant men.'

Later, when they are both mothers, Laura rather less controversially tells her children:

> . . . how her sister stood
> In deadly peril to do her good
> And win the fiery antidote . . .
> For there is no friend like a sister
> In calm or stormy weather;
> To cheer one on the tedious way,
> To fetch one if one goes astray,
> To lift one if one totters down,
> To strengthen whilst one stands.

Christina Rossetti was very close to her only sister, who later became a nun.

The Victorians heralded the era of lifelong sibling attachments. Shortly after the death of Queen Victoria, in 1907, there was a change in a law which seems quaintly historical now, but while it had been in force it had caused considerable distress in some families. The Deceased Wife's Sister's Marriage Act reversed previous law to make it legal for a widower to marry his dead wife's sister. It had been fairly common, after a wife's death, for her sister to move into the family home to take over the care of the children and household. The sister of the wife of the novelist Charles Dickens did so and was remarkably loyal to him. But if a widower fell in love with his late wife's sister they either had to conduct the relationship secretly or move abroad to live openly. Not everyone thought a change in the law was a good idea. The law had been approved by those who thought it stopped husbands lusting after their sisters-in-law while their wives were still alive.

Felicia Skene wrote a novel in 1849 called *The Inheritance of Evil, or the Consequences of Marrying a Deceased Wife's Sister*. The title gives a strong clue as to where she stood on the subject. In this novel the elder sister, Elizabeth, marries Richard but a week before the wedding he meets her sister Agnes who has been away for nearly two years. Agnes is nearly eighteen, and is beautiful.

> Elizabeth turned with a proud delight to present her to Richard, but she stopped short suddenly when she saw his face, whilst an indescribable pang shot through her heart; – her future husband was standing with his eyes fixed on Agnes, gazing at her with a look of the most warm and unqualified admiration, a look such as had never been bestowed on herself.

Women know when their man prefers their sister. Elizabeth's worst fears are realised when her husband falls in love with Agnes. Elizabeth is brokenhearted, becomes sick and dies, fearing that Agnes will usurp her.

One thought alone was present in the mind of Elizabeth Clayton – a thought so torturing and unsupportable that she strove to escape from it with that impotent frenzy which in its full development drives men to the awful crime of self-destruction. She had a RIVAL in her SISTER! The wife, whom she had dreaded would supplant her after her death, would be her, who for two years past had called her husband – brother!

Richard breaks the law and marries Agnes but it all ends in melodramatic tragedy.

By the beginning of the twentieth century there was more awareness of sisterly rivalry. This was especially so in smaller, middle-class families where there was competition for parental attention. As birth rates fell, a new baby could no longer go unnoticed; it deprived other children of their mother's attention. Rather than waiting to reach a marriageable age to become rivals sisters now started bickering about who was the favourite child.

In much of the world the middle of the twentieth century saw political events that tore families apart and separated sisters from their siblings. The Second World War had a larger effect on the civilian population than any war previously. This was especially true for the Jewish population in Europe who were subject to Nazi persecution and genocide. The psychiatrist Sigmund Freud died in Hampstead a few years before four of his sisters, all in their eighties, perished in concentration camps. Jewish parents, fearing what would happen, implored their children always to look after each other. There are many stories about Jewish sisters during the Second World War.

Rena's Promise by Rena Kornreich Gelissen is brutally unsentimental. Through its 266 pages it seems inconceivable that she and Danka, the sister whom she promised her mother she would save, could have survived the beatings, starvations and attempts by Mengele to carry out medical experiments on them in Auschwitz. Every time there were 'selections' for who would live and who would die Rena feared for herself and Danka. In one selection she saw two sisters separated. The one selected to live begged and was allowed to die with her sister. Shortly afterwards Danka refused to eat her meagre rations, which left Rena in despair.

> If we become emaciated we're goners. I try to get her to get her own bowl of soup, but her spirit is dwindling before my eyes. How do I get my sister to want to live? Without that desire there is no way we can survive and I need her just as badly as she needs me.

Rena managed to find out from Danka why she refused to eat: she was terrified of being thrown on to the death trucks without her. Rena reassured her: 'before our parents, I make this oath to you; that from this day on, if you are selected I will join you no matter what. I swear that you will not go on to the trucks alone.' The next morning Danka started taking the soup again. They survived the war and afterwards managed, remarkably, to lead as normal a life as possible. Both Rena and Danka went to live in the United States – it presumably being inconceivable that they would not live on the same continent.

Anne Frank, the young Jewish girl whose diary from her years in hiding during the Second World War is one of the world's most widely read books, also had a sister. Margot, the elder Frank sister, was, according to school friends, the 'special one' who was beautiful and smart. There was undoubtedly sisterly rivalry. Anne resented what she thought was her mother's preference for Margot. As the family suffocated in the confines of their Amsterdam hiding place Anne wrote of everyday family life. Margot was the easier sister, the quiet and obedient one, and Anne the more rebellious sibling. Hiding together made them close for the first time. Anne wrote in her diary that Margot was 'much nicer ... She's not nearly so catty these days and is becoming a real friend. She no longer thinks of me as a little baby who doesn't count.' After being betrayed to the Germans by an informer the girls were sent on the last transport to Auschwitz and managed to stay together, looking after each other, later being moved together to Bergen-Belsen. A few weeks before liberation Margot died. Anne, who was already weak and believed her family were all dead, died a few days later.

After the war a combination of smaller families and mothers who started going out to work changed child-rearing even further. Once divorce rates started rising stepsisters became more common, which didn't dampen sibling rivalry. Since sisters now had lifelong relationships but independent lives it was inevitable that they should compare themselves to each other for even longer. Sisters can use each other as yardsticks against which to measure how successful they are at school, in their careers and relationships. Terrifyingly they can also continue to compete through their children's achievements. The second half of the twentieth century saw psychologists taking a strong interest in sisterly attachment and rivalry, from childhood to old age. Novels presented more complex relationships between sisters, and the depth and everlasting imprint of the bond was expressed poignantly by those who had lost their sisters. Two autobiographical accounts of the loss of sisters from cancer show the intensity and the necessity of this relationship. Justine Picardie's book *If the Spirit Moves You* is a beautiful but harrowing account of the silence she heard and the loss she felt after her younger sister Ruth's death from breast cancer at the age of thirty-three. She writes of visiting her brother-in-law after Ruth's death.

> *... Then, in my dream, I see Ruth standing by the kitchen sink, to show me where I can get a drink of water – and for the first time since her death, I see her not as sick Ruth, dying Ruth, but Ruth as full of life as ever. I know that she is dead – that no one aside from me can see her ghost – but she looks happy, and spirited ... She says nothing, and I am*

silent too, but it doesn't matter. I have seen my sister . . . My sister has seen me.

Alice Bloch's *Lifetime Guarantee* also describes the grief and the hole left in her life by her younger sister Barbara's death. She writes of her feelings when she hears Barbara may have leukaemia. 'She is my sister. I need her. I must know she is somewhere in the world always. Please, she is younger. I have counted on her love, her presence, to the end of my life.' When she visits her in a dreary hospital she recalls how little sibling rivalry there has been between them.

She never blamed me for being the older and more powerful, for soaking up her admiration and never quite returning it in equal measure . . . She never blamed me when I was Mom's favorite for several years. She never blamed me for my lack of acne . . . She never blamed me for bringing her into my world frequently, but never venturing into hers. She never blamed me for carving out my territory first, so that she had to choose from what was left. She never blamed me. I do. I blame myself.

The power of the relationship between sisters has a resonance beyond the family. The reputedly true story of the two 'heroic little sisters of the Grassland' has been investigated for its use as Chinese propaganda by Uradyn E. Bulag, in a paper written while a research fellow at the University of Cambridge. In this story two Mongolian sisters aged eleven and nine were left in charge of their father's sheep. A blizzard swept in and the sisters had to chase after the sheep that were frightened and ran off. They had many hardships. Yurong, the younger, lost one of her boots; they drove off eagles and escaped from a 'class enemy' (a Mongol lord) who tried to steal their sheep. The elder sister, Longmei, was saved from being run over by a train by Comrade Wang, a Chinese signalman who rescued them both and took them to hospital. Both sisters survived (though one was crippled) and all but two of the 380 sheep were saved. The girls' story became enshrined as a heroic Chinese tale. Bulag explains in her paper that children, through the story, were encouraged to hate their Mongolian 'class enemies' and cherish the brave Han Chinese. It was in fact a Mongol man who had saved Longmei and not a Han Chinese man at all, although it took many years for this to be recognised. The propaganda value of the story of the two brave sisters was too high for it to be revised lightly.

If sisters can be used for political means they can also be used for entertainment. Sisters have been prominent in cinema, with films such as *An Angel at My Table*, *Little Women*, *Gas Food Lodging*, *Peppermint Soda* and *Welcome to the Dollhouse* covering a range of sisterly experience from adolescence onwards, predicated on the relationship of sisters being profoundly influential. *An Angel at My Table* is the moving film of the autobiography of Janet Frame, a remarkable woman who lost two of her four sisters in drowning accidents and had severe bouts of depression, one of the worst being linked to the death of one of her sisters. She escaped undergoing brain surgery (a leucotomy) which would have altered her personality irrevocably, because her writing won a prestigious prize just days before the operation was scheduled. The film ends with Janet writing poetry beside her surviving sister's home, having found a way to live with the loss of her other sisters. The more recent film *I've Loved You So Long* (2008) is about two sisters who become estranged following the conviction of the elder one for supposedly murdering her son, who it turns out was terminally ill. It is the rediscovering and rebuilding of the relationship between the sisters that saves them both. The film ends with them living in the youngest sister's house, with her husband, daughter and father-in-law.

The lifelong relationship between sisters, the companionship they may provide for each other, is, however, apparently not recognised by British law. Two elderly sisters, Sybil and Joyce Burden, have lived together all of their lives. Their claim to avoid paying inheritance tax on their home (which would mean it would have to be sold) when one of them dies has been rejected by the

European Court of Human Rights. In a statement issued by their lawyers they said they were struggling to understand why they should have to lose their house because they chose to remain single and look after their parents. Joyce remarked rather poignantly, 'We are sisters and it seems we have no rights at all.' Like all good sisters, they have vowed to go on fighting.

A Sister's Confession

GUY DE MAUPASSANT

Marguerite de Therelles was dying. Although she was only fifty-six years old she looked at least seventy-five. She gasped for breath, her face whiter than the sheets, and had spasms of violent shivering, with her face convulsed and her eyes haggard as though she saw a frightful vision.

Her elder sister, Suzanne, six years older than herself, was sobbing on her knees beside the bed. A small table close to the dying woman's couch bore, on a white cloth, two lighted candles, for the priest was expected at any moment to administer extreme unction and the last communion.

The apartment wore that melancholy aspect common to death chambers; a look of despairing farewell. Medicine bottles littered the furniture; linen lay in the corners into which it had been kicked or swept. The very chairs looked, in their disarray, as if they were terrified and had run in all directions. Death – terrible Death – was in the room, hidden, awaiting his prey.

This history of the two sisters was an affecting one. It was spoken of far and wide; it had drawn tears from many eyes.

Suzanne, the elder, had once been passionately loved by a young man, whose affection she returned. They were engaged to be married, and the wedding day was at hand, when Henry de Sampierre suddenly died.

The young girl's despair was terrible, and she took an oath never to marry. She faithfully kept her vow and adopted widow's weeds for the remainder of her life.

But one morning her sister, her little sister Marguerite, then only twelve years old, threw herself into Suzanne's arms, sobbing: 'Sister, I don't want you to be unhappy. I don't want you to mourn all your life. I'll never leave you – never, never, never! I shall never marry, either. I'll stay with you always – always!'

Suzanne kissed her, touched by the child's devotion, though not putting any faith in her promise.

But the little one kept her word, and, despite her parents' remonstrances, despite her elder sister's prayers, never married. She was remarkably pretty and refused many offers. She never left her sister.

They spent their whole life together, without a single day's separation. They went everywhere together and were inseparable. But Marguerite was pensive, melancholy, sadder than her sister, as if her sublime sacrifice had undermined her spirits. She grew older more quickly; her hair was white at thirty; and she was often ill, apparently stricken with some unknown, wasting malady.

And now she would be the first to die.

She had not spoken for twenty-four hours, except to whisper at daybreak:

'Send at once for the priest.'

And she had since remained lying on her back, convulsed with agony, her lips moving as if unable to utter the dreadful words that rose in her heart, her face expressive of a terror distressing to witness.

Suzanne, distracted with grief, her brow pressed against the bed, wept bitterly, repeating over and over again the words:

'Margot, my poor Margot, my little one!'

She had always called her 'my little one', while Marguerite's name for the elder was invariably 'sister'.

A footstep sounded on the stairs. The door opened. An acolyte appeared, followed by the aged priest in his surplice. As soon as she saw him the dying woman sat up suddenly in bed, opened her lips, stammered a few words and began to scratch the bedclothes, as if she would have made a hole in them.

Father Simon approached, took her hand, kissed her on the forehead and said in a gentle voice:

'May God pardon your sins, my daughter. Be of good courage. Now is the moment to confess them – speak!'

Then Marguerite, shuddering from head to foot, so that the very bed shook with her nervous movements, gasped:

'Sit down, sister, and listen.'

The priest stooped toward the prostrate Suzanne, raised her to her feet, placed her in a chair, and, taking a hand of each of the sisters, pronounced:

'Lord God! Send them strength! Shed Thy mercy upon them.'

And Marguerite began to speak. The words issued from her lips one by one – hoarse, jerky, tremulous.

'Pardon, pardon, sister! pardon me! Oh, if only you knew how I have dreaded this moment all my life!'

Suzanne faltered through her tears:

'But what have I to pardon, little one? You have given me everything, sacrificed all to me. You are an angel.'

But Marguerite interrupted her:

'Be silent, be silent! Let me speak! Don't stop me! It is terrible. Let me tell all, to the very end, without interruption. Listen. You remember – you remember – Henry –'

Suzanne trembled and looked at her sister. The younger one went on:

'In order to understand you must hear everything. I was twelve years old – only twelve – you remember, don't you? And I was spoilt; I did just as I pleased. You remember how everybody spoilt me? Listen. The first time he came he had on his riding boots; he dismounted, saying that he had a message for Father. You remember, don't you? Don't speak. Listen. When I saw him I was struck with admiration. I thought him so handsome, and I stayed in a corner of the drawing room all the time he was talking. Children are strange – and terrible. Yes, indeed, I dreamt of him.

'He came again – many times. I looked at him with all my eyes, all my heart. I was large for my age and much more precocious than – anyone suspected. He came often. I thought only of him. I often whispered to myself:

'"Henry – Henry de Sampierre!"

'Then I was told that he was going to marry you. That was a blow! Oh, sister, a terrible blow – terrible! I wept all through three sleepless nights.

'He came every afternoon after lunch. You remember, don't you? Don't answer. Listen. You used to make cakes that he was very fond of – with flour, butter and milk. Oh, I know how to make them. I could make them still, if necessary. He would swallow them at one mouthful and wash them down with a glass of wine, saying: "Delicious!" Do you remember the way he said it?

'I was jealous – jealous! Your wedding day was drawing near. It was only a fortnight distant. I was distracted. I said to myself: "He shall not marry Suzanne – no, he shall not! He shall marry me when I am old enough! I shall never love anyone half so much." But one evening, ten days before the wedding, you went for a stroll with him in the moonlight before the house – and yonder – under the pine tree, the big pine tree – he kissed you – kissed you – and held you in his arms so long – so long! You remember, don't you? It was probably the first time. You were so pale when you came back to the drawing room!

'I saw you. I was there in the shrubbery. I was mad with rage! I would have killed you both if I could!

'I said to myself: "He shall never marry Suzanne – never! He shall marry no one! I could not bear it." And all at once I began to hate him intensely.

'Then do you know what I did? Listen. I had seen the gardener prepare pellets for killing stray dogs. He would crush a bottle into small pieces with a stone and put the ground glass into a ball of meat.

'I stole a small medicine bottle from Mother's room. I ground it fine with a hammer and hid the glass in my pocket. It was a glistening powder. The next day, when you had made your little cakes, I opened them with a knife and inserted the glass. He ate three. I ate one myself. I threw the six others into the pond. The two swans died three days later. You remember? Oh, don't speak! Listen, listen. I, I alone did not die. But I have always been ill. Listen – he died – you know – listen – that was not the worst. It was afterward, later – always – the most terrible – listen.

'My life, all my life – such torture! I said to myself: "I will never leave my sister. And on my deathbed I will tell her all." And now I have told. And I have always thought of this moment – the moment when all would be told. Now it has come. It is terrible – oh! – sister –

'I have always thought, morning and evening, day and night: "I shall have to tell her some day!" I waited. The horror of it! It is done. Say nothing. Now I am afraid – I am afraid! Oh! Supposing I should see him again, by and by, when I am dead! See him again! Only to think of it! I dare not – yet I must. I am going to die. I want you to forgive me. I insist on it. I cannot meet him without your forgiveness. Oh, tell her to forgive me, Father! Tell her. I implore you! I cannot die without it.'

She was silent and lay back, gasping for breath, still plucking at the sheets with her fingers.

Suzanne had hidden her face in her hands and did not move. She was thinking of him whom she had loved so long. What a life of happiness they might have had together! She saw him again in the dim and distant past – that past for ever lost. Beloved dead! how the thought of them rends the heart! Oh! that kiss, his only kiss! She had retained the memory of it in her soul. And, after that, nothing, nothing more throughout her whole existence!

The priest rose suddenly and in a firm, compelling voice said:

'Mademoiselle Suzanne, your sister is dying!'

Then Suzanne, raising her tear-stained face, put her arms round her sister, and kissing her fervently, exclaimed:

'I forgive you, I forgive you, little one!'

3

Sisters as Rivals

This chapter on sibling rivalry is a long one. I am sorry to say that it was a case of who should be missed out, rather than put in. Sibling rivalry is a common side effect of having either a brother or sister but it is more common in same-sex children who are close in age and can be ferocious where one child is particularly gifted. There are examples from a wide variety of (sometimes surprising) sources. Sisters may become rivals because they want the recognition their sibling has, either from the family or the world outside; because they want the same thing; or because they want to assert themselves. Many of these sisters, it is worth noting, have followed the same careers.

Florence Nightingale is perhaps the most famous Victorian apart from Queen Victoria herself. Generations of schoolchildren imagine her shadow falling from the light of her lamp on to the walls of the Crimean wards and marvel at her selfless heroism. So let us introduce her sister, Parthenope, whose view of Florence was somewhat different.

> I believe she has little or none of what is called charity or philanthropy, she is ambitious – very and would like well enough to regenerate the world with a grand coup de main or some fine institution, which is a very different thing . . . When she nursed me everything which intellect and kind intention could do was done but she was a shocking nurse.

As a character assassination it has the killer blow that only a sister can give. Who else could say that Florence Nightingale was a useless nurse? Parthenope's comments about her sister came from deep childhood jealousies, fanned by a careless father. 'Parthe' was born in 1829 and Florence a year later. Their family was well off, as their father, William Nightingale, had been lucky enough to discover a lead mine. Florence was the more beautiful and intelligent and, although their father started off teaching both girls, she was the more interested in studying. He introduced her to Greek while Parthe ran off and learnt the latest dances with her mother. Florence was noticeably smart; friends would comment on it and she herself felt she had some monstrous precocious quality that made her different from other children. While Parthe (whom Florence also called Pop) adored her younger sister, she felt that her pesky sibling overshadowed her own charm and talents. The sisters fought, only breaking their rivalry when they spent time apart at relatives' houses. During a visit in 1830 when Florence was ten, she wrote pleadingly to Parthenope,

'Pray dear Pop, let us love each other better than we have done, it is the will of God and Mamma particularly desires it.'

However good their intentions were, they were unable to get on. Their relationship wasn't helped by their father's tendency to tell Florence how lazy her elder sister was in the schoolroom. Florence passed the comments on to Parthenope, who wrote to her father in some distress, saying, 'I am prop-

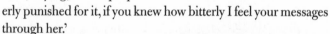

erly punished for it, if you knew how bitterly I feel your messages through her.'

Being party to her father's confidences made Florence feel superior to her elder sister. This wasn't helpful as Florence was feeling pretty superior already. At seventeen, while walking in the garden she felt God calling her to his service. It took some years however for her to realise what this calling was for. In the meantime both sisters came out in society and it was Florence who had and refused the first proposal.

When Florence's interest turned to nursing her family were horrified. In the 1800s nursing was not a profession for ladies. Nurses were mostly untrained, often drunk, and hospitals were squalid. Florence managed to do some training in Germany in a hospital run by Catholic nuns but she returned to a concerted campaign from her mother and sister to discourage her from a nursing career.

By now Parthenope was thirty-one, single and unhappy. She resented both her sister's drive and her ability to attract suitors, and channelled her distress into psychosomatic illnesses that were so convincing that her parents insisted Florence stop what she was doing and nurse her for six months. The six months felt like a lifetime but Florence did try to coax her elder sister out of her moods. 'I have no desire but to die' was Parthenope's catchphrase. Florence felt unable to help. 'What is to become of me,' she wrote. 'I can hardly open my mouth without giving dear Parthe vexation – everything I do or say is a subject of annoyance to her.'

The six months of slavery finally ended and Florence went back to train as a nurse. Parthenope had a hysterical outburst before she went, screaming until she was exhausted. Finally the family took her to see an eminent physician, Sir James Clark, who was brave enough to tell the family what any good doctor should have said twenty years previously. Parthe needed to be separated from her sister or she would never get better. She had, said the good doctor, been overindulged and was utterly self-absorbed.

Florence later wrote of the incident: 'A very successful and justly successful physician once seriously told a sister who was being Devoured that she must leave home in order that the Devourer might recover the health and balance which had been lost in the process of devouring. This person was myself.'

Even their father began to grasp the seriousness of the situation. He wrote,

*I have this day reached the conclusion that Parthe can no
more control or moderate the intensity of her interest in Flo's
doings than she can change her physical form and that her
life will be sacrificed to the activity of her thoughts, unless
she removes herself from the scene immediately.*

When the Crimean War broke out and reports came back of
the terrible care given to wounded soldiers, Florence finally
found her calling. The British government had heard of her
nursing experience and she was offered the post of Super-
intendent of the Female Nursing Establishment of the English
General Hospitals in Turkey. Even Parthenope was sufficiently
impressed to cease hostilities. As the legend of the Lady with
the Lamp travelled back to England, the family realised that
Florence was now a national icon, a ministering angel loved by
the soldiers. Parthenope wrote to her: 'The people love you
with a kind of passionate tenderness which goes to my heart.'

On her return home Florence couldn't escape from either
the public's adoration or her sister's insistence on accompanying her everywhere. She responded by falling ill herself. In 1857
she became so weak she was practically an invalid. This mysterious illness bothered her throughout the rest of her life but
she used it to her advantage. She was too ill, she said, to see any
of her family.

Her illness did not stop her attracting another suitor, Sir
Harry Verney, who was impressed with Florence's work and,
when he met her, fell in love with her. She said she couldn't
marry him but through her he got to know Parthenope. The
elder sister finally achieved something that her sister wouldn't;
she married Henry in June 1858. Harry wrote of his intended

bride, 'In her fortieth year, with the appearance of a lady but without the beauty of her sister Florence.' Ouch.

After their mother died, the sisters became reconciled. Florence took a room in the Verneys' home and as Parthenope became ill with arthritis, she once again nursed her. As the wife of Henry Verney, Parthenope had actually found her forte in life. She became an acclaimed writer, not only rescuing Verney family documents from oblivion by incorporating them into a book but writing essays showing considerable political insight in some of the foremost magazines and journals of the day. By the time she died in 1890 her husband was in no doubt of the role her sister had played in her life. He wrote to Florence,

> *You contributed more than anyone to what enjoyment of life was hers. You and I were the objects of her tender love and her love for you was intense. It was delightful to me to hear her speak of you and to see her face, perhaps distorted with pain, look happy when she thought of you.*

In the last century there is no shortage of examples of sisterly rivalry. Few people realise that the Hollywood actresses Olivia de Havilland and Joan Fontaine were sisters. They preferred it that way. They were, however, the first sisters both to win Oscars (the first in 1941) and to be nominated for best actress in the same year. In her autobiography, *No Bed of Roses*, Joan blames her infant eczema (her mother wrapped her from head to toe in cotton wool until the age of two) for creating a rift between the two sisters. Olivia, who had had her parents' undivided attention for over fifteen months, now had to share it with a white, fluffy, and, by Joan's own account, squalling, puny baby.

Both girls were bright. Olivia was a precocious reader and before the age of six used that skill to terrify her sister. The sisters had been left together unsupervised, and Olivia decided to read from the Bible.

> Listening to her read aloud the Crucifixion from the Bible in mounting gusto, I not only experienced man's inhumanity to man, but that of sister to sister. When she read of the crown of thorns and soldier's stab in the side of Jesus, my screams were heard down the entire row of cottages. Gleefully persisting, Olivia continued reading of Christ's journey up the Via Dolorosa and only when she reached the part when the nails were being driven into his flesh was I rescued by a neighbour from the last cottage in the row. Years later, when I walked the same route that Christ had traversed, the incident returned in all its horror.

Olivia and Joan were competitive from an early age. Joan claims, 'I regret that I remember not one act of kindness from her all through my childhood.' When it came to pursuing acting careers, it was Joan who the family decided would need to change her family name of de Havilland. Olivia got a film contract first, and Joan did the starlet's laundry and tidying and acted as her cab driver until she got her own studio contract. Joan had always felt that Olivia was her mother's favourite and this behaviour confirmed it. But she was also clear that without the rivalry, which their mother encouraged, neither might ever have been so determined to succeed.

Their rivalry peaked in 1941, on the night of the Oscars when both Joan and her sister were nominated for best actress. Joan won.

Now what had I done? All the animus we'd felt towards each other as children, the hair-pullings, the savage wrestling matches, the time Olivia fractured my collarbone, all came rushing back in kaleidoscopic imagery. My paralysis was total. I felt Olivia would spring across the table and grab me by the hair. I felt aged four, being confronted by my older sister. Damn it, I'd incurred her wrath again.

As Olivia tells it (this is a one-sided account, after all), she was mortified by Joan ignoring her congratulations. She waited for her revenge, ignoring Joan's outstretched hand when it was her turn to claim her own Oscar (which Joan presented). The two fell out even further over another traditional area of sibling disagreement – the death of their mother. They fought bitterly over her memorial service, Joan maintaining she was excluded

from the plans until she threatened to go public with a story
that would say the two hated each other and that Olivia had not
invited her to the service. Olivia refuted the story. The two did
not speak to each other and quite likely never spoke again.

Twins are virtually obliged to be best friends, so there is
considerable potential for them to convert to worst enemies.
For fifty years two sisters ruled the daily advice columns of
American newspapers, reaching around two hundred million
people. 'Ann Landers' and 'Dear Abby' were the bylines of
identical twins who wrote their columns in rival newspapers
and whose public bickering was as entertaining as their
answers to readers' problems. The twins, born in 1918, were
too early to benefit from modern childrearing practices, but
even so you'd have to wonder why Abe and Becky Friedman
called their firstborn twin Esther Pauline and the one that
came along seventeen minutes later Pauline Esther. The twins
were dressed alike, were in the same class at school at their
parents' insistence, and were encouraged to share friends and
after-school activities. Until they were married they slept,
curled round each other, in the same bed. Esther became
'Eppie' and Pauline became 'Popo' but they were still
expected to like and dislike the same things. Eppie said of an
early attempt at independence, 'I remember the sense of guilt
I felt, when, at the age of eleven I screwed up the courage to
express a preference for Shredded Wheat over Puffed Rice. I
had been brought up to feel that everything with twins should
be alike.'

When they went to college, it was to the same one; when
they married, it was a double wedding with identical dresses.
Initially they had even wanted the same man, Morton Phillips,

who was the heir to a fortune. Popo won and Eppie was left to find someone else. Perhaps inevitably she went for a man rather lacking in ambition, called Jules Lederer.

There was a geographical separation when Jules and Eppie moved to Chicago. In 1955 Eppie was a bored Chicago housewife and on a whim, having read the 'Ann Landers' advice column in the *Sun-Times*, decided that she wanted to get into the agony-aunt business. The woman who had been writing the column had recently died and Eppie wrote some sample columns and got the job. She immediately rang Popo, not only to tell her but to enlist her help in writing the column.

Popo later said that her replies were the 'snappier'. Certainly she loved being in print and when Eppie's editor found out about the column-sharing and abruptly stopped it, Popo was furious.

Showing that determination has a genetic component, she managed within a few weeks to manoeuvre herself into an agony-aunt role as 'Dear Abby' at the *San Francisco Chronicle*. Eppie's response to her twin's success was initially one of genuine delight, tempered by business concerns. 'I guess it's all right as long as you aren't syndicated outside San Francisco.'

But within three weeks Popo's column was syndicated. Both columns were successful because they were frank and outspoken for their time, covering uncharted territory such as abortions and homosexuality. The competition between them was no longer at the level of who was leader of the first violins in the school orchestra (Popo had been) but was fought out on the pages of national newspapers. Eppie maintained her dignity and largely kept quiet but she was furious with Popo. By the mid-1950s they had stopped talking to each other.

In April 1958 *Life* magazine published interviews
with both sisters enti-
tled 'Twin lovelorn
advisors torn asun-
der by success'.
The interviews
were toe-curling.
Popo accused her sister
of being envious of her
marriage to a millionaire.

Eppie said that Popo was 'just like a kid who beats a dog until somebody looks and then starts petting it'.

The twins did not talk to each other until 1964, when a truce began that lasted for twenty years. It was strong enough that when Eppie's husband asked for (and got) a divorce after he had had an affair, it was Popo whom she called to fly to her side. The truce was almost broken by Popo giving an interview in the *Ladies' Home Journal* in the early 1980s. Popo made the mean remarks that only a sister could make. Eppie, she revealed, had had plastic surgery. If that wasn't cruel enough, she helpfully explained why. Eppie had needed it: she'd done so much damage to her face through crying over her divorce. Popo's remarks allegedly shocked even her husband. 'If these are twin sisters,' he reportedly said, 'I'll take cobras.'

Eppie decided not to cut off her sister on the grounds that they were too old to lose touch. They continued to speak to each other by phone. When Eppie died her niece Jeanne said that Popo 'did not take it well'. It may or may not have been an understatement.

Some sisters wait, perhaps wisely, until the death of their sibling to reveal their rivalry. When English cellist Jacqueline du Pré recorded Elgar's Cello Concerto in E Minor with the London Symphony Orchestra at the age of twenty, music critics the world over were mesmerised. She was vivacious and blonde and wrapped herself around her cello, swaying as she played. Her brilliant career was cut short by multiple sclerosis. She was unable to perform for the last fourteen years of her life and died at the age of forty-two.

After her death in 1987 the music world mourned her. Then along came a biography, written by her sister Hilary and brother Piers, which threw fans and friends of Jacqueline into turmoil. In the book, *Genius in the Family*, Hilary painted a picture of a selfish, tormented soul, who had had an affair with Hilary's husband. What was more bizarre is that she had done so with Hilary's permission.

The story of Hilary and Jackie shows rather bleakly the rivalry of a sister living in the shadow of a genius sibling. The du Prés were a musical family; their mother Iris was a piano teacher and Hilary, three years older than her sister, was started on the piano. Jackie, who quickly became her mother's favourite, chose the cello at the age of four. Hilary was talented but not a genius. It wasn't long before the difference in their abilities became obvious. Hilary was eleven and Jackie eight when they played at the same music festival but while Hilary was enthusiastically applauded, it was Jackie who won the medal for outstanding achievement. Hilary, forgotten in the ensuing uproar, sobbed uncontrollably. For an eleven-year-old the lesson that she would never be as good as her sister was acutely painful. Jackie's brilliance diminished Hilary's more ordinary talent. Hilary would constantly be opening the door of the family home to a procession of people asking, 'How is your wonderful sister?'

As Jackie's career soared, Hilary largely bowed out of performing. She stuck with the musical theme and chose a conductor and musician for a husband, Christopher Finzi, but the couple opted for children and a rustic lifestyle in the country. Hilary watched as Jackie became world-famous, performing with top orchestras and marrying Daniel Barenboim, a pianist and conductor, and comforted herself that she was the sister with the stable family life.

In 1971 Jackie had a psychological breakdown which may have been an early manifestation of multiple sclerosis, as the disease destroys the nervous system. In some distress she moved in with Hilary and her family, and Hilary encouraged her to spend time with Finzi. Even so she was probably surprised to find her sister sneaking into their marital bed one night and trying to sexually arouse her husband. She was, however, accommodating, taking the view that if sex with Finzi would make Jackie well, then she would allow it. That this unusual arrangement reflects strangely on Hilary (how could this have been a good idea?) goes unremarked.

The nine-month affair ended dispassionately but this betrayal, coupled with years of feeling second best, may explain Hilary's oddly dissociated account of her sister's death from multiple sclerosis. When the biography came out and was made into a film, few people bought Hilary's justification of this being 'a love letter to the sister who will always be a part of me'. Her own daughter Clare declared it was a 'gross misinterpretation, which I cannot let go unchallenged'. Clare blamed her father for the affair, painting him as a womaniser who preyed on a vulnerable, disturbed woman.

Did Hilary feel that without Jackie she could have been the special one in the family? Her brother's contribution to his sister's biography is almost negligible. This is a story about the intense rivalry between sisters, played out with a painful lack of insight by the main protagonist. We know very little of how Jackie felt about her only sister. Rather tellingly she once told Carol Easton, who wrote a biography of Jackie in 1989 two years after her death, that her siblings resented her. Fortunately she was spared knowing the full extent of that resentment.

Sometimes it is hard to gauge the true extent of sisterly rivalry. The highly acclaimed writers A. S. (Antonia) Byatt and her younger sister, Margaret Drabble, are both so talented that any rivalry should be unnecessary. But the rivalry seems to be rooted in their childhood, in a discontented mother who was extremely bright and went to Cambridge University but lived in Sheffield at a time when women were expected to be housewives. Margaret depicts her in a fictionalised account in her novel *The Peppered Moth* as an angry and tragic figure. Margaret has said her mother encouraged them to be rivals, which may explain their relationship as adults. She remembers trailing after her elder sister, desperate for attention that was not forthcoming. Antonia, in turn, recalls a childhood where she was mostly silent and fearful of the outside world and spent many days confined to bed with asthma, reading books. Their mother told both girls at an early age that they would go to Cambridge. So, dutifully, both of them did, Antonia gaining a first-class English degree and Margaret doing even better with a starred first. There was some inevitability about Margaret's first book, *A Summer Birdcage*, being about two sisters and their rivalry. Antonia countered this in 1967 with *The Game*, also about two sisters, one an Oxford don, the other a best-selling novelist, who muse over their strange upbringing and rivalry. The don kills herself after she is depicted in a satirical way in her sister's novel.

The authors' rivalry is unlikely to be fatal but it has rumbled on. Most disputes seem to be about their fictitious accounts of events that happened to them both. Antonia said publicly that she was upset by *The Peppered Moth* because it was 'someone else's version of my mother'. Margaret said that she had not read her sister's bestselling novel *Possession* because it featured places they visited on childhood holidays. There is a pervasive sense of childhood unhappiness that has never been resolved.

In an interview in the *New York Times* in 1991, Antonia spoke frankly about her relationship with her sister, revealing the cause and extent of their rivalry.

> My mother liked Maggie much better. They could fight and scream and slam doors at each other and then feel better . . . I thought [Maggie] was likely to be more successful because she was more outgoing. And because she wanted to outdo not only my mother but me. I set a very high standard, and she did. We were close and still are, in a very basic way, but I always feel threatened by her.

Sibling rivalry does not have to be destructive. So this chapter ends with an uplifting example. Venus and Serena Williams have scooped the major titles in tennis, often competing against each other. Their father, Richard, who groomed them for championship tennis at an early age, allegedly to get them out of the ghetto, was not shy about saying in public which sister he thought was the more able. 'Serena will be better than Venus. She's more aggressive. She has a better all-around game.' Serena, who is fifteen months younger than Venus, is recognised as being the better player but the sisters have not fallen out over it. They have always shared a home together (early on they often shared a bed in more cramped circumstances) and they share a motto for whenever they play tennis: 'If you can't do it for you, do it for me. And die on the court!'

The sisters have always been close. When Serena forgot her lunch money at school, Venus would go hungry so she could eat; when they went out for a meal Serena would have whatever her elder sister ordered. When Serena first beat her sister it was much harder for her to deal with than when she had been beaten by Venus. This was, she says, 'because Venus has always taken care of me my whole life – she's the ultimate bigger sister.' Their closeness even led to accusations that they agreed off court who would win whenever they played against each other.

But it is Serena who has kept on winning, pulling off a major comeback when she won the Australian Open after not playing for sixteen months and at eighty-one in the world rankings. Venus, sitting at home, could hardly bear to watch. But she had sent emails and phoned her sister several times a day throughout the tournament giving her tips on how to beat her opponents.

There were five Williams sisters (three from their mother's previous marriage, although they dislike any of them being referred to as half-sisters) but the eldest, Yetunde, was shot and killed as an innocent bystander in a gang incident in 2003. The sisters were shattered but did their best to support each other. Serena went to court and read out a statement when her sister's killer was convicted, saying in a simple understatement that the murder had been 'unfair' on their family. The tragedy may have made her more determined to win. It was to Yetunde that Serena dedicated her win at the Australian Open.

There is a story about Venus's win over her sister at the US Open in 2001 which was reported at the time and epitomises their relationship. When victorious players come to the net to shake hands, they may say 'Thanks' or 'It was a close game'. Venus hugged Serena and just said, 'I love you.'

Julie Showalter on her sisters

I am the oldest of three sisters, cannot remember a time when I did not have sisters. Karen was born when I was eighteen months old, Billy Sue less than a year after her. From the start, I was mother's little helper, a role which grew into telling my sisters about Santa Claus and sex, which I thought entitled me to tell them what to do. Billy Sue went along with this system. Karen didn't.

When I was twelve, Karen lined the three of us up in front of a mirror. 'Look,' she said. 'Look at our mouths. Julie, yours is too big. Billy Sue, yours is too little. Now see how mine is right in the middle, just the right size for a mouth.' She moved on to eyebrows.

Karen has always attributed any of her character flaws to having been the middle child. 'Middle child syndrome,' she will shrug to deflect criticism, even now when she's fifty years old. From where Billy Sue and I stood, being in the middle looked pretty good – not too young to go after my boyfriends, not too old to steal Billy Sue's. And there was the mouth – medium size, just right. And the eyebrows, thicker than mine, thinner than Billy Sue's.

In a family that apportioned traits like fairies at a christening, Karen was the pretty one. She was also the funny one, the one who could do the impossible – make Daddy laugh. She was the one who drove Mother crazy.

We moved the year I was in eighth grade, so Karen and I hit a new junior high together. That's when I found out she was the popular one, the vivacious one, the one the boys wanted to walk to class and the cheerleaders wanted to share lockers with.

I was the smart one with glasses and no style. The one that teachers noticed but that other students didn't.

The rivalry that began when she was two weeks old and I bit her toe intensified and it took on purpose. We would protect our turf. She could never be smart and I could never be pretty or popular. We made sure of it.

When we weren't fighting, we did each other favors. I'd do her homework, dashing off in ten minutes a set of algebra problems that would have taken her hours, in the process establishing her reputation as the one who cheated. Teachers held her up to ridicule. 'How can your homework be so good and your tests so bad?' 'Obviously you can do the work if you try.' And worst of all, 'You certainly aren't like Julie.'

Teachers knew I helped her cheat. But they were never angry at me. They saw the way she ignored me in the halls. They heard her giggle with her boyfriends when I walked by.

In high school, she tried to teach me to dance. Tried until the night before the prom when she declared me hopeless. 'You'll never get it,' she said. 'There's a look you have to have and you don't have it.' The next night we double-dated in matching dresses our Granny had made. I sat at the candle-topped card table in the gym, too embarrassed to dance and expose myself as not having the look, feigning interest in the Wonderland by Night decorations, pretending it didn't bother me that Karen took turns dancing with our two dates.

Sibling rivalry, at least our version of it, is not so simple as wanting what the other has. It's not wanting the other to have what you have. It's wanting the other to want to be like you. It's proving every moment that you're nothing like her.

I married the week of my nineteenth birthday. Young, but not scandalously young. Karen married six weeks later – seventeen and a half. Married in the church where my wedding had been. Wore my dress and veil. Sat before the wedding smoking a cigarette wearing my dress and veil.

Six weeks later her husband got drunk and beat her. I invited her to stay with my husband and me while her broken heart mended. If my husband got up to get a Coke, she said, 'I waited on Phil hand and foot.' When I brought home hamburgers for dinner, she said, 'I cooked all day for Phil.' One evening she volunteered, 'Phil and I made love for two hours every night.' When I found my husband with his arm around her comforting her while she cried, I sent her back to Mother to take care of.

There's a certain amount of score-keeping.

She had the first failed marriage, but I had the second. And the third. But both my failed marriages lasted a respectable length of time. So who's ahead there?

She had our parents' first grandchild. A month later, I adopted a three-month-old daughter, so I had the oldest grandchild.

I spent six years in analysis. She straightened herself out for free with a self-help book and Oprah. You be the judge – who should feel smug?

These things don't change. At thirty she had her breasts enlarged. And suddenly, my breasts, which had been in the middle, not tiny like hers or huge like Billy Sue's, were the smallest. I no longer had the right size breasts.

At forty I flew home from our father's funeral weeping hysterically. Why? Because an hour earlier Karen had entertained assembled friends and relatives with a story about me picking my nose in first grade.

And now. I'm fifty-one, she's fifty. Last month our niece, Billy Sue's older daughter, got married. As I fretted about what I'd wear, my husband said, 'Do you really think all eyes will be on the aunt of the bride?'

Not all eyes, but two.

What I want from her is the following: I want her to admit I looked better at that wedding. I want her to admit I danced better. I want her to admit my life is better than hers. I want her to admit that she could never have done the things I've done.

And she admits these things, some of them, but she doesn't do it right. I have a PhD, was the only one of us to go to college. I've held impressive jobs with big titles. What does she say about me? 'Julie is the most successful of all of us. She married a doctor.'

I am a writer who has had some success with stories of our childhood. What does she say? 'Anyone could write those stories. I'll tell you the stories and you just put in the right words.'

4

Elder and Younger Sisters

There are some sisters whose relationship is defined by who came first. Who is the elder sister and who is the younger. The established patterns of childhood can last a lifetime; the elder one who still feels she has to pay when she goes out with her younger sister, the younger one who wonders if she will ever be as grown-up as her older, more glamorous sister. You can argue it either way who has the trickier time. The elder sister may be the first to have the mobile phone, the pierced ears and the parties, but she will have felt the disruption of the younger sister who comes along, usurping her as the only girl in the family and asserting her right to her mother's lap. Parents are usually stricter with the elder child and have higher expectations of them, while the younger, in her elder sister's eyes, 'gets away with murder'. The elder may be given responsibilities when her younger sister is born, such as getting her own clothes ready for school, or, if she is old enough, being asked to babysit.

If you are the elder you may have been irritated by your younger sister ruining your games when your friends came round, by her hanging around you and messing up your cherished possessions. You may see your younger sister as an embarrassment and later in life worry that you treated her as such. I see some of this played out among my three daughters, how the younger two so want their elder sister to be as enchanted with them as they are with her. Often, with incredible sweetness, she is. But how hard it is for them when everything they try to do is done so much better by her. How excluded they feel when I have a more adult discussion with her about things they don't understand. Their elder sister will try to correct their manners at the dinner table, she will help them with their homework and music practice, and sometimes this is done with love and patience and sometimes with exasperation. She thinks they should mind her as much or as little as they mind me, but they don't. They have taken away my time from her, which may be a good thing, but she reminds me gently that while I endlessly ferry them around I have less time for her. She still needs a mother.

Psychologists say that elder sisters have an innate sense of responsibility and self-righteousness. They may be bossy and domineering to their younger sisters. The youngest has the envied position of never being ousted as the baby of the family and is usually the most cuddled and most assured of her parents' love. If there are only two sisters, the second may try to catch up the elder sister, coming up behind in the hope that in some sphere of life she will overtake her. Elder sisters may watch their backs anxiously but more often they sail through childhood, too busy to see their younger sister as a person in her own right until they are both more independent, sometimes not until adulthood.

But accidents of birth do not always obey convention, and there are many younger sisters who are responsible and from an early age support their elder sister. Some women have been deeply influenced, both in their achievements and their family life, either by being an elder sister or by having one.

When Margaret Mead's work *Coming of Age in Samoa* became a bestseller in 1928 few people realised she had honed her anthropological skills on her younger sisters. Margaret was born in America in 1901, the eldest of five children, and as the first was much loved and wanted. She knew this because she was always told by her besotted Quaker parents, 'There's no one like Margaret.' Her mother, Emily Fogg Mead, was a sociologist who filled thirteen notebooks describing Margaret's development and, worn out by this, managed only four on her brother Richard who was born two years later. Margaret had two sisters, Elizabeth, seven years younger, and Priscilla, who was nine years younger. Another child, Katherine, born after Richard, had died aged six months, a tragedy that Margaret had nightmares about for years. Margaret, like many elder sisters, had mixed feelings about her siblings, and remembered with shame blaming the toddler Elizabeth for a cut that she

herself inflicted on her nose with a forbidden penknife. It was, she wrote in her autobiography *Blackberry Winter*, 'a cardinal sin I have never forgotten'.

It was Margaret's grandma who encouraged her to take notes on her sisters' development. Her grandma pointed out the differences in how the girls behaved and spoke: Priscilla mimicked the shouts and oaths hurled up the backstairs by their servants; Elizabeth was at a stage where she spoke in her own poetic way. Margaret became fascinated by the contrasts between her younger sisters, in a rather maternal way. Her observations were, she said, a labour of love. Elizabeth was loving and devoted, Priscilla more self-centred but disconcertingly open about being so. Margaret notes, 'She would pay someone a compliment and then remark, "But I only told you so you would take me along."' In describing their family relationships when she was twenty-two (having had some years to come to terms with her childhood), Priscilla said, 'Dick was Dadda's favorite, Elizabeth was Grandma's favorite, Margaret was everybody's favorite . . . I was Mother's favorite, but Mother didn't count for much in our house.'

What most puzzled Margaret, the future anthropologist, was the effect that being forced to be right-handed had on her two sisters. Both were naturally left-handed and in the 1920s this was considered abnormal. Their grandmother, after seeing a psychologist, insisted they use their right hands. Priscilla did fine and a short time later won a spelling competition; Elizabeth started stuttering and was barely able to write. Margaret mulled over why one sister should react so differently from the other. In a typical eldest-sister way she was proud of her sisters, Elizabeth for her artistic ability, Priscilla for her beauty and pragmatic approach to life. In *Blackberry Winter* she reflects on the relationship between sisters.

Thinking about the contrasts between my sisters led me also to think about the other women in my mother's family and of the way in which, generation after generation, pairs of sisters have been close friends. In this they exemplify one of the basic characteristics of American kinship relations. Sisters, while they are growing up, tend to be very rivalrous and as young mothers they are given to continuous rivalrous comparisons of their several children. But once the children grow older, sisters draw closer together and often, in old age, they become each other's chosen and most happy companions. In addition to their shared memories of childhood and of their rela-

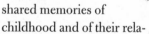

tionships to each other's children, they share memories of the same house, the same homemaking style. And the same small prejudices about housekeeping that carry the echoes of their mother's voice as she admonished them, 'Never fill the tea-kettle from the hot-water faucet,' and 'Wash the egg off the silver spoons at once,' and 'Dry the glasses first.' But above all, perhaps, sisters who have grown up close to one another know how their daydreams have been interwoven with their life experiences.

The Mead sisters' feelings for each other were mutual. Elizabeth must have been thinking of her own sisters when she said,

> If you tell your sister to go to hell in twelve different languages and you need a quarter, you can say, 'I need a quarter.' And she'll give it to you. A friend may say I don't want to see you again. And a friend you can give up. You can't give up on a sister. You were born with them and you die with them. Or they die and leave you and you feel absolutely discomforted.

Margaret knew how to be an elder sister. She encouraged her sisters to pursue careers that she thought suited them and provided them with unstinting support. As the first to leave home and have a career, Margaret was the person that her sisters sought advice from. Not only did she have the wisdom of an older sibling, she had the anthropological experience to make her advice more useful than the average sister's insights might have been.

When Elizabeth had her first experience of sexual activity, it was her elder sister, who was working in Samoa, that she wrote to. Margaret wrote a sweet and touching reply: 'It was a nice boy whom you like, and nothing that need worry you ... The thrills you get from touching the body of another person are just as good and legitimate thrills as those you get at the opera.' She finishes her letter by saying, 'I am very proud of the way you are able to think thru the problems which life brings you – and of the way you meet them. And I consider it a great privilege to have you tell me about them.'

Priscilla wrote to ask her sister's opinion on weaning, even though Margaret was not to have a child herself for another year. Her sister advised her wisely not to feel guilty about whatever she decided to do.

Through her anthropological work Margaret developed strong views on sibling rivalry. It was, she felt, incredibly hard for elder siblings to be displaced from their exclusive position with their mother, whatever the society they were born into. She felt enormous compassion for an elder child who sees her mother helping her younger sibling do things that she is no longer praised for doing, but expected to get on and do them for herself. Margaret never had to deal with sibling rivalry as a mother. She had been told she could not have children, but managed to have a daughter with her third husband, Gregory Bateson.

The responsibility she felt for her siblings and the role she had in making sense of what happened in the family was particularly poignant in the aftermath of Priscilla's suicide in 1959. Priscilla's daughter wrote to her aunt a decade after the tragedy asking for information about her mother, who had had a history of depression. Margaret offered to put together some letters and photographs for her. 'You are quite right,' she wrote. 'Your mother was very brave, and beautiful.'

However many friends and colleagues Margaret had, and there were many, Elizabeth, who outlived her, had a special place in her heart. It was Elizabeth whom Margaret would call on to babysit when young Mary Catherine Bateson was unwell. But even so she always felt she was partly a mother to her younger sibling. Elizabeth in many ways informed and defined

Margaret's optimistic view of life. In a letter to a psychoanalyst friend, Margaret wrote,

> She is not only my favourite sister but as a child she came to stand to me as a sort of symbol for the beauty of life, because she was born three years after my older little sister had died, and became in a sense that other baby reborn. From that experience I drew such a confidence that life holds a sequence of good things that the most precious experience will not be lost, but will come again, that it has in a way patterned my whole life, and definitely surrounded Elizabeth with a special halo.

Simone de Beauvoir, the French philosopher and feminist, was two and a half years old and initially jealous when her younger sister Hélène was brought home. But this jealousy

turned into relief that she was no longer an only child and could finally have someone to play with. The de Beauvoirs had set their hearts on a boy and never really tried to hide their disappointment at having girls, but the birth of another daughter confirmed Georges de Beauvoir's intentions to give Simone the same education as a man. Their mother, Françoise, took some comfort in hoping the younger sister would be more malleable, as neither she nor her husband could control Simone's tantrums. Françoise had bitterly resented her own younger

sister and expected, perhaps even wanted her girls to fight, but they somehow managed to develop a close, enduring relationship. Their deep affection for each other was astounding as their parents were forever raving about Simone's intellect and ignoring Hélène's abilities. Simone's fierce love for her sister protected her from some but not all of the hurt.

Both sisters led creative lives. Simone became famous for her philosophical and political writings as well as for her relationship with the existentialist Jean-Paul Sartre. *The Second Sex*, published in 1949, was a powerful analysis of the oppression of women and became essential reading for feminists worldwide. Its premise was that women are not born but made. Hélène became a highly acclaimed painter but she was always Simone's sister and as such she was subject to people's hostility. Hélène too was a feminist; she spoke up for the right to abortion and supported refuges for battered women at a time when this stance was unfashionable. Simone said of her once, 'It is hard to be the sister of someone so famous, you are the butt of so much humiliation and jealousy.' The sisters were close throughout their lives. After Simone's death, Hélène plaintively asked what would happen to her now, having lost the sister who had protected her for seventy-six years.

Simone's autobiography, *Memoirs of a Dutiful Daughter*, describes her sister and their relationship beautifully, even if Simone herself sounds somewhat self-obsessed at times. When Hélène read it she was profoundly moved because she had never fully realised the extent of her sister's love for her.

We called her Poupette; she was two and a half years younger than me. People said she took after Papa. She was fair-haired, and in the photographs taken during our childhood her blue eyes always appear to be filled with tears. Her birth had been a disappointment, because the whole family had been hoping for a boy; certainly no one ever held it against her for being a girl, but it is perhaps not altogether without significance that her cradle was the centre of regretful comment. Great pains were taken to treat us both with scrupulous fairness; we wore identical clothes, we nearly always went out together; we shared a single existence, though as the older sister I did in fact enjoy certain advantages. I had my own room, which I shared with Louise, and I slept in a big bed, an imitation antique in carved wood over which hung a reproduction of Murillo's *Assumption of the Blessed Virgin*. A cot was set up for my sister in a narrow corridor. While Papa was undergoing his army training, it was I who accompanied Mama when she went to see him. Relegated to a secondary position, the 'little one' felt almost superfluous. I had been a new experience for my parents: my sister found it much more difficult to surprise and astonish them; I had never been compared with anyone: she was always being compared with me. At the Cours Désir the ladies in charge made a habit of holding up the older children as examples to the younger ones; whatever Poupette might do, and however well she might do it, the passing of time and the sublimation of a legend all contributed to the idea that I had done everything much better. No amount of effort and success was sufficient to break through that impenetrable barrier. The victim of some obscure malediction, she was hurt and perplexed by her situation, and often in the evening she would sit crying on her little chair. She was accused of having a sulky disposition; one more inferiority she had to put up with. She might have taken a thorough dislike to me, but paradoxically she only felt sure of herself when she was with me. Comfortably settled in my part as elder sister, I plumed myself only on the superiority accorded to my greater age; I thought Poupette was remarkably bright for her years; I accepted her for what she was – someone like myself, only a little younger; she was grateful for my approval, and responded to it with an absolute devotion. She was my liegeman, my alter ego, my double; we could not do without one another.

I was sorry for children who had no brother or sister; solitary amusements seemed insipid to me; no better than a means of killing time. But when there were two, hopscotch or a ball game were adventurous undertakings, and bowling hoops an exciting competition. Even as I was just doing transfers or daubing a catalogue with water-colours I felt the need of an associate. Collaborating and vying with one another, we each found a purpose in our work that saved it from all gratuitousness. The games I was fondest of were those in which I assumed another character; and in these I had to have an accomplice. We hadn't many toys; our parents used to lock away the nicest ones – the leaping tiger and the elephant that could stand on his hind legs; they would occasionally bring them out to show admiring guests. I didn't mind. I was flattered to possess objects that could amuse grown-ups; and I loved them because they were precious: familiarity would have bred contempt. In any case the rest of our playthings – grocer's shop, kitchen utensils, nurse's outfit – gave very little encouragement to the imagination. A partner was absolutely essential to me if I was to bring my imaginary stories to life . . .

I owe a great debt to my sister for helping me to externalise many of my dreams in play; she also helped me to save my daily life from silence; through her I got into the habit of wanting to communicate with people. When she was not there I hovered between two extremes: words were either insignificant noises which I made with my mouth, or, whenever I addressed my parents, they became deeds of the utmost gravity; but when Poupette and I talked together, words had a meaning yet did not weigh too heavily upon us. I never knew with her the pleasure of sharing or exchanging things, because we always held everything in

common; but as we recounted to one another the day's incidents and emotions, they took on added interest and importance. There was nothing wrong in what we told one another; nevertheless, because of the importance we both attached to our conversations, they created a bond between us which isolated us from the grown-ups; when we were together, we had our own secret garden . . .

What I appreciated most in our relationship was that I had a real hold over her. The grown-ups had me at their mercy. If I demanded praise from them, it was still up to them to decide whether to praise me or not. Certain aspects of my behaviour seemed to have an immediate effect upon my mother, an effect which had not the slightest connection with what I had intended. But between my sister and myself things happened naturally. We would disagree, she would cry, I would become cross, and we would hurl the supreme insult at one another: 'You fool!' and then we'd make it up. Her tears were real, and if she laughed at one of my jokes, I knew she wasn't trying to humour me. She alone endowed me with authority; adults sometimes gave in to me; she obeyed me.

One of the most durable bonds that bound us together was that which exists between master and pupil. I loved studying so much that I found teaching enthralling. Playing at school with my dolls did not satisfy me at all; I didn't just want to go through the motions of teaching: I really wanted to pass on the knowledge I had acquired.

Teaching my sister to read, write and count gave me, from the age of six onwards, a sense of pride in my own efficiency. I liked scrawling phrases or pictures over sheets of paper: but in doing so I was only creating imitation objects. When I started to change ignorance into knowledge, when I started to impress truths upon a virgin mind, I felt I was at last creating something real. I was not just imitating grown-ups: I was on their level, and my success had nothing to do with their good pleasure. It satisfied in me an aspiration that was more than mere vanity. Until then, I had contented myself with responding dutifully to the care that was lavished upon me: but now, for the first time, I, too, was being of service to someone. I was breaking away from the passivity of childhood and entering the great human circle in which everyone is useful to everyone else. Since I had started working seriously time no longer fled away, but left its mark on me: by sharing my knowledge with another, I was fixing time on another's memory, and so making it doubly secure.

Carly Simon, the singer and songwriter, was, like Simone de Beauvoir, deeply affected by her position in her family. There were four Simon siblings, Joanna, Lucy and Carly, who all sang, and Peter, their younger brother, who went into photography. But it is Carly, the youngest, whom most people have heard of. The sisters were brought up in a musical family and sang round the piano in not altogether harmonious circumstances, as their mother was apparently highly critical of their singing. Joanna, the eldest sister by three years, became an opera singer; Lucy sang for a while with Carly and then gave up (although she resumed a solo career later), leaving the youngest sister to outshine them all. Carly explained her relationship with Lucy in an interview for Elizabeth Fishel's landmark book *Sisters: Love and Rivalry inside the Family and Beyond*:

> I was very preoccupied with Lucy for ten years from the time I was about ten to twenty, I really lived vicariously through her for a long time, until I had some kind of a life that I liked of my own. I was just fascinated by Lucy and her friends and wanted to be like them and wear everything they wore and look like them and feel like them and act like them. I identified so much with her that I almost lost myself in the bargain.

Carly surpassed both of her sisters' achievements. Her song 'You're So Vain' was an anthem for women for many years. Lucy, who returned to music after having children, never came close to her sister's success and must have suffered from being compared to her. In her interview with Fishel, Carly said that she tried to minimise her success by telling her sisters that she has no time for herself, the implication being that fame and fortune are overrated, so there's no need for them to be jealous. Her song 'Two Little Sisters' captures beautifully the significance of sisterhood.

Dr Ann Robinson on her sister

It was a sign of the changing times. When my brother and I were born in the early sixties, we were given standard English names. By the time my sister came along in 1966, my Anglo-Jewish parents must have felt secure enough in their ethnic identity to give her a single Hebrew name, Malka. Luckily for Malki, as she is known, they eschewed its English equivalents, 'Queenie' or 'Regina'. Imagine having to cope with that in the playground! Ironically, with her blonde curls and blue eyes, Malki was the most Aryan-looking baby the family had ever produced.

Family photos show a very beautiful, smiley baby. But I have few early memories of my sister because I was too caught up fighting my brother, Mo. My appetite for sibling rivalry, competition for parental approval and need to dominate were sated in my relationship with him. Poor Mo. At his wedding, he said he'd always been the 'loser sandwiched between two domineering sisters'. A good line but untrue on two counts: he's not a loser, and Malki has never been domineering. In fact, after an early career as a management consultant, she retrained as a mediator – a role to which she is fantastically well suited.

Perhaps I would have fallen out with Malki when she became a teenager, as sisters often do when the younger one starts to encroach on the elder sister's territory. But our dad died when she was just twelve and so normal family rules of engagement ceased to apply.

Our mum blamed Dad's death on the economic recession of the 1970s. It was more likely the cigarettes, fatty foods, complete lack of exercise and genetic predisposition that delivered three successive heart attacks, the last of which killed him at the age of forty-eight. My mum was just forty-three.

I was plunged into an emotional vortex; a sense of bewilderment and abandonment piled on top of normal teenage angst and self-pity. I flunked my A levels and had to retake. I was totally self-absorbed. Our dad's death probably intensified my instinct to protect my baby sister and try to show her a good time. But it was only years later that I wondered how the loss of our dad affected her and how she felt about spending her teenage years living alone with my mum while my brother and I left home.

But Malki has a quite remarkable generosity of spirit that gives her a much more positive take on life than my more gloomy nature. She doesn't dwell on loss, grief or abandonment. Instead, she has stories of a trip to Paris that I arranged for us and a painting and fancy dinner that I bought her when she turned twenty-one. The same generosity of spirit means that she involves our mum in the lives of her children to an extent that I could never manage. I was too pig-headed, and maybe too selfish, to ask for much help. Malki gets our mum in for all manner of childcare jobs. Picking up, dropping off or holding the fort

while she pops out. I can see now that everyone benefits:
Malki, the kids and perhaps most of all our mum, who
thrives on being needed, even if she does look fit to crumble after a few rounds with the four-year-old.

Of all her endearing characteristics, it is in her role as
aunt to my children that I have recognised just how much I
love her. My brother, sister and I all reproduced the same
family pattern that we were born into. We each had a girl,
then a boy, then another girl. Malki
had her first child after my
youngest was born so she
had a few years to hone
her skills as an auntie.
She proved a natural
hit, organising excit-
ing birthday-present
options for my kids.
She'd send a card
with three options –
say ice-skating,
bowling or cinema
outing. Whichever
option the child ticked
would be agreed on and
Malki turned up at the
appointed time, in a glamorous car
and with a big smile on her face. She never failed to deliver
and my kids love her for her attention to detail and her
unforced interest in them.

Four years ago a cataclysmic event happened to our family. My eldest daughter, Zoe, became ill with leukaemia. She

was ill for two years and died before her sixteenth birthday. The loss of Zoe is the prism through which my every thought and memory is now refracted.

While Zoe was ill and in the two years since she died, my sister has reflected my pain in her eyes. I have seen her love of me, her aching sadness and her own terror about the possibility of losing a beloved child. I have, at times, found it hard to look into her eyes because of what I see there. It is too painful for either of us to discuss yet. Malki has handled me with unfathomable tact, understanding and compassion during this time. She kept coming to the hospital with Starbucks coffee and my favourite biscotti while Zoe and I were incarcerated there. She phones, pitches up and includes my younger daughter in outings with her kids. She is gentle and warm and her usual endearing self.

When I have healed enough, I will tell her how sorry I was to bring such sadness into her life. And I will tell her that though my life is blighted, having her as a sister is an enduring source of companionship, comfort and celebration.

5

Beloved Sisters

Some sisters have such close relationships, lives that are so indivisible, that they are worth a chapter of their own. Historically this was more likely to happen when unmarried women had their most intimate adult relationship with a sister. Such relationships could be intense and enduring. The sisters here are mostly literary ones, perhaps because it is easy for us to know about their closeness because they wrote about it. But what they wrote was not always what they meant. The Brontë sisters are simply extraordinary, Jane Austen and her sister Cassandra are endearing but annoying because so little of the real relationship survives to be pored over, and the Stephen sisters, Virginia and Vanessa, were locked in a doomed but passionate relationship.

In Haworth Parsonage, long after the adults had gone to bed, the three Brontë sisters would walk round and round the dining-room table reciting their latest writings and critiquing each other's efforts. Charlotte, Emily and Anne were original, wonderful authors but if they hadn't been sisters they might not have been famous; their closeness gave them enormous confidence and self-belief. Charlotte was always the driving force, the ambitious one who insisted they get their work published.

Early in life the girls had had a series of tragedies. Their mother had died when they were young, leaving them in the

care of their father Patrick, a clergyman, and Aunt Branwell, who was God-fearing but none the less affectionate. More maternal support came from the elder Brontë sisters, Maria and Elizabeth. Maria encouraged her younger sisters and Branwell, their only brother, to make up games based on stories from newspapers. Their closeness was intensified by their lack of friends outside the family.

Poverty initially kept Patrick from formally educating his children but he found he could afford one of the cheap boarding schools that sprung up in the 1820s, the Clergy Daughters'

School. Maria and Elizabeth went first, followed rapidly by Charlotte, then Emily. For those who have read *Jane Eyre*, the brutal regime of Lowood Hall is modelled on the Clergy Daughters' School. Maria suffered more than most. She had tuberculosis and one day, despite being ill, was struggling to get dressed when she was dragged in front of the girls by a teacher who rebuked her loudly for her 'dirty ways'. Charlotte later captured this haunting moment in *Jane Eyre*, when Helen Burns is cruelly treated even as she is dying. Helen is drawn as a child of such purity, kindness and self-sacrifice that Charlotte told her publisher, 'I have exaggerated nothing there. I abstained from recording much that I remember respecting her, lest the narrative should sound incredible.'

Patrick was too late to do anything but bring Maria home to die, which she did on May 1825, just eleven years old. Even as Maria was being nursed at home, Elizabeth was showing signs of the same disease and was sent home from school to die just a month later. Patrick, terrified for his younger daughters, rushed up to the school to bring them home. They never went back.

Charlotte was now the eldest sister and she felt inadequate for the job. In her mind her elder sisters had always been superior to herself. When told many years later that someone from the Clergy Daughters' School had remembered her, Charlotte refused to believe it.

They might remember my eldest sister Maria: her prematurely developed and remarkable intellect, as well the mildness, wisdom and fortitude of her character, might have left an indelible impression on some observant mind among her

companions. My second sister, Elizabeth, too may perhaps
be remembered, but I cannot conceive that I left a trace
behind me.

All of them felt the loss of the older girls, which reverberated
throughout their writing; Charlotte and Emily's main characters are orphans.

The four remaining siblings had always enjoyed reading and
acting out plays, but now they started writing in volume,
Branwell and Charlotte creating fantasy stories that evolved
into a world called Angria, and Emily and Anne breaking away
to write about the kingdom of Gondal. Their stories were elaborate – Charlotte in particular wrote long, luscious descriptions – but they were also an opportunity for the children to
poke fun at each other. The world of Gondal was less sophisti-
cated than that of the elder siblings and Charlotte was rather
scathing about the unimaginative conversations its characters
had, for example, about what would happen if they got their
clothes dirty.

In 1845 the sisters were living with their father at Haworth
Parsonage and Branwell had returned home in disgrace, having had an affair with the mother of a pupil he was tutoring.
Branwell began a three-year decline into alcoholism and opium
dependence, but he announced he was writing a novel. Her
brother's aspirations prompted Charlotte to have a similar
idea. She found a notebook of poems that Emily had written
but never shown to her. In a preface to Emily's novel
Wuthering Heights she described the moment of discovery:

One day, in the autumn of 1845, I accidentally lighted on a
MS. volume of verse in my sister Emily's handwriting. Of

course, I was not surprised, knowing that she could and did write verse: I looked it over, and something more than surprise seized me – a deep conviction that these were not common effusions, nor at all like the poetry women generally write. I thought them condensed and tense, vigorous and genuine.

Charlotte decided to get her sister's work published, in a volume of poetry that would also include poems by Anne and herself. But she had to push her sister into agreeing and Emily insisted on assumed names; they chose Currer, Ellis and Acton Bell because they sounded ambiguously masculine (it still wasn't considered feminine to write). Charlotte finally found a publisher but they sold only two copies. Fortunately this did not deter them. Emily went on to write *Wuthering Heights*, Anne wrote *Agnes Grey*, and Charlotte wrote *Jane Eyre*, which was the first to be published. It was the most critically acclaimed of the novels.

Fortunately the sisters did not seem to be competitive about their writing. They had their own styles, just as they had very different personalities. But it's not clear what the sisters were really like because it was left to the one who lived longest, Charlotte, to describe them. Anne, the youngest, would have been a genius had she been part of any other family. As it was she wrote in a very different way from her sisters, largely disapproving of their masculine characterisations which she thought made attractive heroes out of immoral men. Her books have a moral tone that may have been the influence of the observant Aunt Branwell. While there seems to have been no sibling rivalry about their relative successes as novelists, Anne's next novel, *The Tenant of Wildfell Hall*, is a direct response to her sisters' unpalatable heroes. In this novel, which depicts alcoholism and domestic violence, the villain may be handsome but he is still a flawed, bad man who does not change. In what would have been remarkable in Victorian England, his wife leaves him, taking their young son with her.

Charlotte must have felt the rebuke. The novel's anti-hero was criticised as coarse and brutal but Anne's powerful writing was praised and the book quickly sold enough to warrant a second edition. Charlotte, however, found it hard to come to terms with her baby sister writing about such adult themes:

> *The choice of subject was an entire mistake. Nothing less congruous with the writer's nature could be conceived . . . She had, in the course of her life, been called on to contemplate, near at hand, and for a long time, the terrible effects of talents misused and faculties abused: hers was naturally a sensitive, reserved, and dejected nature; what she saw sank very deeply into her mind: it did her harm. She brooded over it till she believed it to be her duty to reproduce every detail . . . as a warning to others.*

Charlotte did not mean to diminish her sister by these words, but to have her remembered as a good Christian woman who didn't understand the dark side of human life. Anne was, in fact, no shadow of her sisters but rather an early feminist who could write convincingly about brutish husbands.

The death of Branwell from drugs and alcohol, which involved his family watching him convulsing and crying out in distress, interrupted any further publishing attempts.

Charlotte could not really forgive Branwell for disappointing her. With terrible honesty she wrote of how they had all had such pride and hopes for him and how he had been, by virtue of being a man, their father's favourite.

The loss of Branwell made Charlotte ill (it was the delicate Anne who remained strong, even answering Charlotte's letters for her) and she was slow to realise that Emily and Anne were both suffering from tuberculosis. She eventually confided her unease to her friend Ellen Nussey, but still felt terrified and alone. Emily, who had a cough and chest pain and was growing thinner daily, refused to see a doctor. This may have been because she did not want to suffer the usual painful and useless remedies of the day.

For her sisters, watching her body shaken by coughing fits and hearing her panting for breath, the despair they felt was terrible and relentless. Emily tried to do the everyday things she had always done, comb her hair, feed the dogs and continue to sew. Charlotte wrote later:

> She sank rapidly. She made haste to leave us. Yet, while physically she perished, mentally she grew stronger than we had yet known her. Day by day, when I saw with what a front she met suffering, I looked on her with an anguish of wonder and love. I have seen nothing like it; but indeed, I have never seen her parallel in anything. Stronger than a man, simpler than a child, her nature stood alone.

Emily died on 19 December 1848 at the age of thirty.

Anne, the youngest, was now in the final throes of consumption. She had seen how much the family had struggled because Emily had refused all help, and so agreed to the indignities of medical treatment. She tried to appear calm and resigned for the sake of her sister and father but she was desperately frightened by her diagnosis. Anne's real torment is shown in a poem she wrote after hearing how ill she was. The first stanza shows her fear and distress at knowing she will die like Branwell and Emily.

> A dreadful darkness closes in
> On my bewildered mind
> O let me suffer & not sin
> Be tortured yet resigned

The poem is written as a dialogue between Anne and God in which she says it's unjust for her to die.

> I hoped that with the brave and strong
> My portioned task might lie.

After Anne's death Charlotte felt that this poem did not fit her portrayal of Anne as a stoic, resigned to her fate. She edited this poem heavily and removed the first four stanzas to make the poem read as though Anne was reconciled to death. Charlotte could not bear to think her sister was in turmoil.

It was Anne who tried to comfort Charlotte. As she lay dying she managed to say weakly from her sofa, 'Take courage Charlotte! Take courage!' Charlotte described the scene to her publisher, William Smith Williams, who had become a friend:

> . . . *she died without severe struggle – resigned – trusting in God – thankful for release from a suffering life – deeply assured that a better existence lay before her . . . Her quiet – Christian death did not rend my heart as Emily's stern, simple, undemonstrative end did – I let Anne go to God and felt He had a right to her. I could hardly let Emily go – I wanted to hold her back then – and I want her back now – Anne, from her childhood seemed preparing for an early death – Emily's spirit seemed strong enough to bear her to fullness of years – They are both gone – and so is poor Branwell – and Papa has now me only – the weakest – puniest – least promising of six children – consumption has taken the whole five.*

In her preface to *Wuthering Heights* Charlotte painted a picture of Emily as the vigorous, passionate sister, Anne the paler, more passive version. After Anne's death Charlotte, who had

lost one brother and two siblings in just ten months, wrote a
poem about the loss of her youngest sibling.

ON THE DEATH OF ANNE BRONTË

> There's little joy in life for me,
> And little terror in the grave.
> I've lived the parting hour to see
> Of one I would have died to save.
>
> Calmly to watch the failing breath,
> Wishing each sigh might be the last;
> Longing to see the shade of death
> O'er those beloved features cast.
>
> The cloud, the stillness that must part
> The darlings of my life from me;
> And then to thank God from my heart,
> To thank Him well and fervently;
>
> Although I knew that we had lost
> The hope and glory of our life;
> And now, benighted, tempest-tossed,
> Must bear alone the weary strife.

Charlotte went on to finish her novel *Shirley* but the impact of
losing her siblings is noticeable. The manuscript of *Shirley* is a
mess of rewritten passages and even names have been changed.
In comparison *Jane Eyre*, written with the support of her sisters, is a cleaner, more confident manuscript. With the death of
Anne there were no longer any siblings to walk with round the
table late at night, critiquing each other's work.

*

It is precisely because Jane Austen's best friend was her sister
Cassandra that we know so little about one of the best-loved
novelists in English history. Cassandra called Jane the 'sun of
my life, the gilder of every pleasure'. After Jane's death she
destroyed many of the letters that Jane had sent her and edited
others; one of their six brothers also did his share of burning,
with the aim of controlling the outside world's view of their
sister. Out of the estimated three thousand letters sent by Jane
(mostly to her sister) only about 160 remain, many of them
funny, with beautiful observations, but none of them remotely
emotional, controversial or terribly personal. It is tempting to
take this to mean the vast majority contained such inflamma-

tory material as would have thrown the gentle Jane Austen into a different light altogether. At the time of her death her novels, *Pride and Prejudice* in particular, had attracted some attention; Cassandra may have worried that in the future her sister's life might have been examined by more predatory folk than literary critics.

Cassandra Austen was born in 1772, Jane's older sister by three years. The two were close confidantes from an early age. Neither felt close to their mother and this made them even more mutually reliant. When Cassandra was sent to a boarding school in Reading, Jane, although only ten, insisted on going too. Her mother remarked that 'if Cassandra's head had been going to be cut off, Jane would have hers cut off too'.

There is some evidence from another source as to what the sisters were like. When Cassandra was fifteen and Jane twelve, they went to stay with their great-uncle in Sevenoaks in Kent. Their cousin Philadelphia wrote to her brother, describing them.

> *As its pure nature to love ourselves, I maybe allowed to give the preference to the eldest, who is generally reckoned a most striking resemblance of me in features, complexion, and manners . . . The youngest (Jane) is very like her brother Henry, not at all pretty and very prim, unlike a girl of twelve; but it is hasty judgement which you will scold me for.*

Jane, had she known, might have been hurt by this (what twelve-year-old girl does not want to be pretty?) but she always thought Cassandra was superior to her in every way. This included, perhaps improbably, her writing. Jane always maintained that her sister was 'the finest comic writer of the present age'.

The girls, like those in Jane Austen's novels, were expected to marry well, although the Austens seem to have had a more relaxed view than some families. Cassandra was engaged to Thomas Fowle, a military chaplain, but after he died of yellow fever while ministering in the Caribbean in 1797 she decided to embrace a spinster's life. Jane seems to have had a flirtation with Thomas Lefroy, an Irish relative of an older friend of hers, Anne Lefroy, which could have become serious had Jane's family been wealthy (they were not). Jane seems to have confided only in Cassandra, who was away at the time. On one level she writes flippantly: 'At length the day is come on which I am to flirt my last with Tom Lefroy, and when you receive this it will be over. My tears flow at the melancholy idea.' Cassandra at one point scolded her for her casual behaviour.

Their single status meant not only that they relied on each other (and that their most intimate relationship was with each other), but that they were called upon by various family members to help out, for example when there was sickness or a new baby or even just boredom. In the absence of modern transport, visits were often two or three months long, which is why so many letters were written between the sisters. Jane wrote to amuse her sister: 'Charles Powlett gave a dance on Thursday, to the great disturbance of all his neighbours, of course, who you know, take a most lively interest in the state of his finances, and live in hopes of his being soon ruined.' In a later letter she describes Mrs Powlett as 'everything that the neighbourhood could wish her, silly and cross as well as extravagant'. Cassandra would undoubtedly have smiled and replied in a similar fashion.

Although the letters came thick and fast there was competition for Jane's literary attention. During the 1790s Jane wrote close-to-complete drafts of her novels *Sense and Sensibility*, *Pride and Prejudice* and *Northanger Abbey*. For some reason, never explained, she set them aside for a decade.

Not only do sisters feature prominently in her novels but for their time they are groundbreaking in being characters who move the plots along. They are not stylised but real and raw; there is rivalry and bitterness, as well as unselfish love and deep understanding. In *Emma* her heroine is defined by not having a sister (hence her lack of self-awareness) and then by finding an unsuitable surrogate. There is rarely the perfect sisterhood in her novels that Jane came close to with Cassandra. In *Sense and Sensibility* Elinor, the elder sister, is level-headed and rational; Marianne, the younger, is passionate to the point of being uncontrolled and injudicious. They don't confide the anguish they feel in their love lives to each other until the end of the book, and only then do they understand each other. In *Pride and Prejudice* there are five sisters, the relationship of the eldest two most likely to resemble Jane's own relationship with her own sister. Elizabeth Bennet is spirited, if too quick to judge; her elder sister Jane (who was surely based on Cassandra) is beautiful, and generous about everyone. The other sisters all have equally clear characters: Mary is grave and self-important, Lydia strong-willed and heedless, and Kitty too easily influenced by Lydia. The range of characterisations in the novels must have come from the society that both Jane and Cassandra observed almost constantly, with sisters jostling for partners and dowries.

After their father died the Austen women moved to a sleepy

village in Hampshire where Jane wrote every day, revising her previous drafts, and Cassandra ensured she was relieved of household tasks. Jane began to publish her books in 1811; *Sense and Sensibility* was followed by *Pride and Prejudice*, both of which sold well. In 1816 Jane began to feel unwell. By mid-April 1817 she was confined to bed and secretly wrote her will, making her sister her executor and leaving her almost everything. On 17 July she had a seizure and was agitated for some time afterwards. The doctor administered laudanum and Cassandra sat by her bedside. Jane died quietly and her sister closed her eyes. Cassandra describes Jane's death and her own feelings in a letter to their niece, Fanny Knight.

Since Tuesday evening, when her complaint returned, there was a visible change, she slept more and much more comfortably; indeed, during the last eight-and-forty hours she was more asleep than awake. Her looks altered and she fell away, but I perceived no material diminution of strength, and, though I was then hopeless of a recovery, I had no suspicion how rapidly my loss was approaching.

I have lost a treasure, such a sister, such a friend as never can have been surpassed. She was the sun of my life, the gilder of every pleasure, the soother of every sorrow; I had not a thought concealed from her, and it is as if I had lost a part of myself. I loved her only too well – not better than she deserved, but I am conscious that my affection for her made me sometimes unjust to and negligent of others; and I can acknowledge, more than as a general principle, the justice of the Hand which has struck this blow.

You know me too well to be at all afraid that I should

suffer materially from my feelings; I am perfectly conscious of the extent of my irreparable loss, but I am not at all over-powered and very little indisposed, nothing but what a short time, with rest and change of air, will remove. I thank God that I was enabled to attend her to the last, and amongst my many causes of self-reproach I have not to add any wilful neglect of her comfort.

She felt herself to be dying about half an hour before she became tranquil and apparently unconscious. During that half-hour was her struggle, poor soul! She said she could not tell us what she suffered, though she complained of lit-tle fixed pain. When I asked her if there was anything she wanted, her answer was she wanted nothing but death, and some of her words were: 'God grant me patience, pray for me, oh, pray for me!' Her voice was affected, but as long as she spoke she was intelligible.

I hope I do not break your heart, my dearest Fanny, by these particulars; I mean to afford you gratification whilst I am relieving my own feelings. I could not write so to any-body else; indeed you are the only person I have written to at all, excepting your grandmamma – it was to her, not your Uncle Charles, I wrote on Friday.

Immediately after dinner on Thursday I went into the town to do an errand which your dear aunt was anxious about. I returned about a quarter before six and found her recovering from faintness and oppression; she got so well as to be able to give me a minute account of her seizure, and when the clock struck six she was talking quietly to me.

I cannot say how soon afterwards she was seized again with the same faintness, which was followed by the sufferings she could not describe; but Mr Lyford had been sent for, had applied something to give her ease, and she was in a state of quiet insensibility by seven o'clock at the latest. From that time till half-past four, when she ceased to breathe, she scarcely moved a limb, so that we have every reason to think, with gratitude to the Almighty, that her sufferings were over. A slight motion of the head with every breath remained till almost the last. I sat close to her with a pillow in my lap to assist in supporting her head, which was almost off the bed, for six hours; fatigue made me then resign my place to Mrs J. A. [her sister-in-law] for two hours and a half, when I took it again, and in about an hour more she breathed her last.

I was able to close her eyes myself, and it was a great gratification to me to render her those last services. There was nothing convulsed which gave the idea of pain in her look; on the contrary, but for the continual motion of the head, she gave one the idea of a beautiful statue, and even now, in her coffin, there is such a sweet, serene air over her countenance as is quite pleasant to contemplate . . .

The last sad ceremony is to take place on Thursday morning; her dear remains are to be deposited in the Cathedral. It is a satisfaction to me to think that they are to lie in a building she admired so much; her precious soul, I presume to hope, reposes in a far superior mansion. May mine one day be re-united to it!

Cassandra's loss was extreme; she had, after all, lost her life's companion. She wrote to Fanny again after the funeral. She had been too busy organising the service to be felled by misery but as the procession left the house she felt, she said, 'I had lost her for ever.'

As Jane's executor Cassandra was not going to fail her sister by being unbusinesslike. In less than six months she arranged for *Northanger Abbey* and *Persuasion* to be published. She also set about burning her sister's letters and depriving biographers of many of the thoughts of Jane Austen. It was an action that Jane would undoubtedly have thanked her sister for.

Virginia Woolf and her sister Vanessa Bell had a more troubled relationship than Jane and Cassandra. They did not always approve of each other, they were competitive and sometimes fell out but they loved each other passionately. Vanessa, as the elder sister, was a surrogate mother for her sister after their mother died.

Virginia was born in 1882 and was one of four children of the Stephen family. Vanessa and Thoby were older and Adrian the youngest. In his biography of Virginia, Quentin Bell explains that despite the two sisters competing for Thoby's attention, they were 'passionately fond of each other'. Virginia thought Vanessa beautiful: 'She reminded me always of a sweet pea of a special flame colour.' She admired her sister's honesty, the responsibility she took for them as children, her practical nature and sensibility. 'She not only loved her sister,' says Quentin Bell, 'but, it would seem, loved the affectionate relationship between them.' For many years, growing up, Virginia felt insecure whenever Vanessa fell asleep before she did.

The relationship was not without some serious scrapping. In the nursery Virginia would annoy Vanessa by running her nails down a rough wall. She called her sister the saint, which stuck with the grown-ups, much to Vanessa's irritation. The girls grew up surrounded by Victorian literary society and were taught classics and literature by their parents. Early on the sisters decided that to avoid competition, Vanessa would be the artist and Virginia the writer. When their mother Julia (who had three children from a previous marriage) died in 1895, Virginia was thirteen. She wrote of her mother's death as being 'the greatest disaster that could happen'.

Their father was inconsolable and it was Stella, his step-daughter, who initially looked after Virginia and Adrian before Vanessa, who was only fifteen, assumed the responsibility for the household. Virginia became extremely anxious after her mother's death and had the first of her mental breakdowns. Within two years Stella, whom the girls were very fond of, also died, followed eight years later by their father. Vanessa was relieved at their father's death because she was exhausted from looking after him and the household, but for Virginia it was another deeply unhappy period. After the funeral the sisters escaped to Italy together but while Vanessa had a wonderful time, flirting with friends of her brother Thoby in Paris and looking at the works of painters she had always admired, Virginia was troubled and quarrelsome. When she returned home Virginia had her first major depressive illness and went off to be cared for away from London in the home of a friend. It was perhaps because she had seen how ill her sister was that Vanessa was always so concerned about her. In her many letters to Virginia (and Vanessa wrote nearly every day) she pleads for Virginia to eat properly and showers her with advice.

*My monkey, do be sensible . . . You have such a horror of
making a fuss about yourself, but really it's much wiser to
recognise the fact that you aren't strong in some ways and to
look out for them, and I should have a great respect for you if
you did.*

Vanessa sold the family home in Kensington and provided a
new one for her brothers and for Virginia, who moved in when
she was better. Their new home was more vibrant than their
last. When Thoby went off to university he made friends who
would become members of their 'Bloomsbury set' and brought
them home to meet his sisters. It was not quite the done thing
to have young men mixing with young ladies in the small
hours of the morning but Vanessa and Virginia were not
inclined to be conventional. In the midst of their exciting new
life, Thoby died. His death changed for ever the relationship

between Vanessa and Virginia. Both sisters were traumatised but whereas Virginia looked immediately to her sister for support, Vanessa, in a move unforeseen by anyone, agreed to marry Clive Bell, who had been courting her. Although it's unlikely that Virginia would have approved of anyone, she really didn't approve of Clive. He was not only unworthy in her eyes but his family were horribly respectable. In the aftermath of the loss of Thoby, Virginia felt that Vanessa, who had long been like a mother to her, was now dead to her too. Thoby's death propelled Virginia into writing seriously and it is probably no coincidence that Vanessa responded in her own way by having a baby a year after the wedding.

It was the baby that further changed the relationship between the sisters. Perhaps fuelled by jealousy that Clive and now the baby had taken her place in Vanessa's affections, Virginia began openly to flirt with Clive. Vanessa's husband was flattered, especially since his wife was preoccupied with their son. Vanessa was deeply hurt but she never confronted Virginia. The two did not have a love affair but they became confidants and shut Vanessa out. Virginia began to send her affection to her sister through Clive, in semi-sexual and rather unkind references, asking him to 'Kiss her, most passionately, in all my private places – neck, and arm, and eyeball, and tell her – what new thing is there to tell her? How fond I am of her husband?'

Vanessa remarked that her sister's letters read like love letters. Some years later when Vanessa had a lover and Virginia was married to Leonard Woolf, there was still a tension between them, with Vanessa never quite trusting her sister and Virginia feeling forever culpable and guilty. But the sisters were always writing to each other and their support was mutual and unwavering. Virginia throughout her life had not only loved Vanessa but also her sister's children. She lived through the death of her beloved nephew Julian and through Vanessa's desperate love for the artist Duncan Grant, who, although he became her lover, was gay and unable to commit to her.

Vanessa in turn worried about Virginia's bouts of depression and tried to protect her, even from a distance. In March 1941 she wrote to her firmly, having been worried that her last book, *Between the Acts*, had left her depressed, since she was complaining of headaches and unable to sleep. She told Virginia that she had to be sensible (Vanessa's favourite exhortation to her sister) and needed to rest, if only because she, Vanessa, depended on her.

Since this is the last letter Vanessa wrote to her sister, before Virginia loaded her coat pocket with heavy stones eight days after it was sent and waded into the river to drown, it has been forever analysed. Was Vanessa too tough in her tone? Should she have been more sympathetic? The day before her suicide Vanessa had spoken to her on the phone about coming round for tea and Virginia had sounded pleased. Vanessa had simply not realised how desperately ill her sister was.

As Virginia prepared to end her life she wrote two suicide letters and left them both neatly in the kitchen, in blue envelopes. One was to Leonard, telling him how much she loved him; the other was to Vanessa.

> *You can't think how I loved your letter. But I feel I have gone too far this time to come back again. It is just as it was the first time, I am always hearing voices, & I know I shan't get over it now . . .*

I can hardly think clearly any more. If I could I would tell
you what you and the children have meant to me. I think you
know. I have fought against it but I can't any longer
Virginia

The closeness of some sisters, their ability to know what each
other feels – or at least to want to know – is not something confined to historical sisters. It may seem flippant to talk about the
pop singer Kylie Minogue and her less famous singing sister
Dannii within a few sentences of Virginia and Vanessa but really
it isn't. Anyone who saw Dannii's face and heard her speak after
Kylie was diagnosed with breast cancer will have seen a woman
who would have done anything to relieve her sister's anguish.

This is probably true for lots of sisters, but Kylie and
Dannii's case is different in that they began their careers as
child stars in Australian soap operas, with Dannii overshadow-
ing her sister by presenting a weekly television talent show. But
after that it was always Kylie and the media was inevitably comparing them. Kylie reinvented herself after the soap opera
Neighbours as first a pop star and then a sex symbol. But in
2005 she was diagnosed with breast cancer and Dannii rushed
to Australia to be with her. Little of their family life gets into the
media but their relationship seems to be well grounded. Dannii
has said philosophically of being compared to her sister,
'People will always try to compare you to somebody.'

John Holborow on his sisters

On the face of it there's nothing very remarkable about this family gathering. It is a glorious sunny autumn day. My wife, my five-year-old son and I join my two older sisters for Sunday lunch. Caroline, the eldest of the three of us, has invited us all to her home, and Emma, a year her junior, is visiting London with her Italian partner. One of Caroline's two sons is home from boarding school with his girlfriend; his two younger sisters play with my son with varying degrees of enthusiasm. We drink and make small talk before sitting down to lunch. It is the sort of ordinary family get-together that must be happening in countless homes across the world this weekend. The sort of informal gathering that is a regular occurrence in most families.

But this is a very irregular occurrence in my family. In fact, this is the first time my sisters and I have been together for over five years. My son has met my sister Caroline only three times before today. He has never met his oldest first cousin before. This has nothing to do with geography – Caroline and I live less than two miles from each other. The distance between me and my sisters is a very different thing. The small talk is not easy-going chatter born out of familiarity with the themes of each other's lives; it is simply all we can manage when there are so many things unspoken, and so many arguments hanging unresolved.

In the weeks before this important lunch I reflect even more than usual on how my sisters and I ended up where we are. As usual I do not have any straightforward answers. We grew up in a happy home, I think. The photo albums and the memories I have are full of smiles and laughter, images and well-worn anecdotes from holidays together with my parents, play with mutual friends and family pets. It was never idyllic, but it felt good all the same. Then my mother died of cancer when I was fourteen. Her illness was not allowed to interrupt my education, nor Caroline's. I was driven back to school, and my O levels, the day after her funeral: Caroline drove herself back to university and her finals. Is that what broke our family, and splintered the ties between Caroline, Emma and me? Or was it that my father remarried quite quickly? Or was it all born of the much older jealousy that two older sisters might understandably feel towards a younger brother who was their father's favourite?

What is clear is that through the twenty years between the slow death of my mother and the very sudden death of my father, my sisters and I remained on generally friendly terms, without ever quite achieving that special sibling intimacy I think I see, and envy, between some of my friends and their siblings. There were arguments, recriminations and entrenched differences, but there was also friendship, warmth, and times when we helped each other, and sought out each other's company, just for its own sake. As the youngest I always felt proud of my two successful sisters and believed in their unconditional love, even if I was forgetful of birthdays and slow to reply to invites. I took it for granted that they would be there for me because I felt that ultimately when the chips were down I would be there for them; just because, well, that's what brothers do for sisters. Isn't it?

But then the events of a single day left my family in pieces. We gathered to divide up my father and mother's belongings. My stepmother was finally, after a couple of years' grace, selling the large house she and my father had retired to. It was not our family home, but it was filled with all the assembled belongings of our family. Together, my sisters and I had agreed to encourage, persuade and then finally demand that our stepmother relinquish her grip on these things and the capital tied up in the house. I had acted as the spokesman for what I felt was the agreed agenda of the three of us children, and helped overcome the reluctance of an ageing lady to give up her home and many of the things which had been hers for many years.

The day was already going to be a sad occasion where emotions would inevitably run high and where conflicting currents of grief and nostalgia would clash with material considerations about what was worth what and who got which special, fondly remembered item. But add to that the tension of this reluctant sale. Then throw in, for good measure, the announcement I made over coffee that Sophie, my wife, was pregnant. And finally baste it all in the long-held and unspoken resentments which finally found their voice on that day. The result was a searing, vicious row at the close of the day. It started off on narrow premises but it soon escalated. It was nasty and cruel. We knew what to say to hurt each other, as only brothers and sisters can know. Tears were shed, doors were slammed, and Caroline left. Not long after so did I.

For months I raged at my sisters. One for what I perceived as her dishonesty, her manipulation, co-opting me to drive her agenda then disowning it. Somewhere else I raged at my other sister for not doing enough to mend what was broken, and deep down resented her for being at home when my mother was dying. I raged at my father for the vagaries of his will, for putting stepmother ahead of children, for leaving a landscape which permitted this to happen. And then over time I started to wonder what I had lost. Just because they were my sisters did I really need to like them too? I painted a layer of false indifference over the broken raw edges of what had happened. And then I became a father and found a reason for renewed anger: how could my elder sister deny my son an aunt, cousins, family? Emma, ever the middle child of three, found herself a go-between, telling brother and sister what each was doing, never quite comfortable with either. My sisters were largely lost to me, even if I studiously observed the birthdays of nephews and nieces now – a kind of remembrance of the pain of what I had lost, what my sisters had cost me and my son.

But I mourned the loss without ever acknowledging that grief. It had been easy to dismiss, or suppress, because no mother or father survived to bang our heads together and show me what a fool I was for forsaking the incomparable experience that being a brother to a sister is.

In the end it was my sisters who showed me, that autumn day, what it is to have sisters again. They had some help: Sophie insisted on the occasion, unwilling to let any more time pass where her son missed out on knowing his family. And my son embraced them with his trust and unfettered love. It was in many ways a strange, stilted occasion. Nothing that had been unspoken was spoken, no issues discussed, no apologies or explanations offered. But it is undoubtedly a beginning.

And that's how I came to watch my sisters and our nephews and nieces gather around the partially cleared table and play a game together. My boy sat very close to Caroline, his aunt, turning to whisper questions into her ear, focused intently on the new, unfamiliar game, but safe and relaxed in the knowledge that she was there besides him. I saw what a fabulous mother she is, how gentle and beautiful her children are.

We have a way to go, my sisters and I. Communication remains stilted. I have not yet found a way to tell them how extraordinary it felt to see one rest her hand gently on my son's shoulder, another pick him up to listen to his urgent questions. But I will.

6

Campaigning Sisters

Women have campaigned throughout history for rights for others as well as for themselves. They have fought for the abolition of slavery, for equal rights and for better education for all. Some of the most famous of these women have been sisters, supporting each other in the face of social disapproval and isolation. One sister usually influenced the other but without each other, neither might have had the impact they did have. In America there were among others, the Grimkés and the Adams sisters; Britain had the Pankhursts. But way before them, in AD 12, there were the Trung sisters of Vietnam.

The Trungs are not just any old campaigning sisters, but heroines credited with saving what is now Vietnam from being swallowed up by China. The sisters were the daughters of a Vietnamese lord, and the eldest was called Trung Trac, the youngest Trung Nhi. The sisters became rebellious from an early age, presumably from seeing Chinese troops mistreating the Vietnamese people. The Vietnamese version of their story (which differs from the Chinese account) says that Trung Trac's husband made a stand against the Chinese who were beginning a programme of more forceful assimilation and was killed. In AD 39 the sisters responded by gathering a rebel army of eighty thousand, of which many of the generals were women. The rebellion was successful with the army defeating the Chinese forces and reclaiming territories including the ancient political capital where the Trung sisters were proclaimed co-queens and established a royal court. Their triumph, however, did not last as the Chinese returned in AD 42 to recapture the region. The sisters fought bravely but were defeated. To avoid being killed by the Chinese they did the 'honourable' thing and committed suicide, reputedly by drowning in a river. The sisters have been remembered as heroines in Vietnam, with temples named after them and an annual holiday dedicated to them.

Less dramatically, Abigail Adams, the second First Lady – she was married to John Adams, the second president of the United States – was in her own way a rebel. Without the help of her sisters she would have struggled to cope. Like the Grimké sisters (below) she was ahead of her time, opposing slavery and promoting rights for women. Her parents, William (who was a minister of the Church) and Elizabeth Smith, had three daughters: Mary, born in 1741, followed by Abigail three years later, then a son called William in 1746 before a final daughter, Elizabeth, in 1750. The three sisters were quickly labelled by their parents: Mary was the quiet one who looked after everyone, Abigail was the wilful volatile one and Elizabeth the brainy one. In the tradition of many families with multiple daughters, they had a saying that compared Mary with Abigail: 'A thread would govern one, a cable would be necessary for the other.'

Mary was the first to marry, followed by Abigail, who was quick to interfere when Elizabeth started courting. She had a number of suitors and Abigail accused her of trifling with men's feelings, a charge which made Elizabeth furious. It was only when Abigail became pregnant nearly a year later (Elizabeth had got married in the meantime) that the two made up, sufficiently so for Abigail later to leave her sons with her younger sister while she went abroad to join her husband. It was Mary who did most of the support work for Abigail. As John's political career flourished, Abigail relied on her sister to look after their estate and often the children while she followed John round the country or on overseas duties. Abigail was always deeply thankful, as well she might be, and the sisters exchanged news. Mary's letters were full of local gossip; in return Abigail wrote of world politics and fashions. Their letters were confidential, although they would each read out parts to other family members. When, during his term as president, John Adams was caught opening and reading one of Mary's letters, his wife was unimpressed. 'He has not opened any since I scolded so hard,' she wrote some time afterwards.

As sometimes happens with three sisters, there was one, Elizabeth, who felt left out. Abigail visited Mary more often, admittedly because they lived closer to each other, but Abigail had a habit of promising to see Elizabeth and not turning up. In February 1789, after another failure to show, Elizabeth wrote a heartfelt letter to her sister. 'In the full assurance of seeing you here, we had made all the preparations in our power. Perhaps you may say that would not be much.' She pointed out how she had invited guests to meet her, made up beds and set the table. 'So you may fancy to yourself what a curious figure we made to our neighbors.' She ended her letter by reminding Abigail of their father's views on the importance of family. 'If you had one drop of his blood stirring in your veins, you would have pushed forward and not have failed coming.'

In fact both sisters missed seeing Abigail as her husband became more prominent politically. Elizabeth forgave Abigail, who was still too busy to visit, and the two continued to write to each other, sharing their interest in politics and in particular the rights of women. When John Adams became president, the sisters continued to write to each other, Abigail being warned by her husband to 'hold her tongue' and not to discuss confidential matters. Abigail found this challenging. She asked her sisters to make sure she didn't change once she became First Lady. If she did show signs of grandeur, she urged her sisters, 'with the utmost freedom acquaint me with it'.

The sisters were quietly confident that Abigail would sail through the business of being First Lady; they were more concerned about her husband. Mary warned him that his speeches sounded as if he was flattering the public, Elizabeth that they were too complicated. Abigail agreed and poor John was told that the sisters all felt his inaugural speech had been difficult to understand. The president clearly listened to their advice; Mary sent him a letter some time after, congratulating him on explaining himself much more clearly. Abigail herself sought to influence him into considering the rights of women. She believed passionately in the right of women to education and to own property after marriage. In a letter to her husband in 1776 she wrote,

And, by the way, in the new code of laws which I suppose it will be necessary for you to make, I desire you would remember the ladies and be more generous and favorable to them than your ancestors. Do not put such unlimited power into the hands of the husbands. Remember, all men would be tyrants if they could. If particular care and attention is not paid to the ladies, we are determined to foment a rebellion, and will not hold ourselves bound by any laws in which we have no voice or representation.

When Adams replied that he could not change the status quo, in a teasing letter in response, he was treated to a serious reply from Abigail:

. . . you must remember that arbitrary power is like most other things which are very hard, very liable to be broken; and, notwithstanding all your wise laws and maxims, we have it in our power, not only to free ourselves, but to subdue our masters, and without violence, throw both your natural and legal authority at our feet.

The sisters were split up when Mary died, followed by Elizabeth in 1815. Abigail, who had expected Elizabeth to outlive her, was heartbroken. The loss of her sisters affected her deeply. 'I stand alone,' she told her son, John Quincy (who was later to become president himself), 'the only scion of the parent stock – soon to be levelled with the rest. Would to God that I felt myself equally worthy with those who have gone before me, but I fear I am but an unprofitable servant.' Abigail died in 1818; it wasn't until 1920 that women in America were given the right to vote.

No one would have predicted that the Grimké sisters, Sarah and Angelina, would take up the abolitionist cause. They were born in South Carolina, Sarah in 1792 and Angelina in 1805, where their father was a plantation owner and Supreme Court judge who was also an enthusiastic slave-owner. Sarah, however, never approved of slavery. At the age of five she saw a female slave being whipped and, as the story goes, ran away and was found on the wharf, begging a sea captain to take her anywhere that did not have slavery. She was twelve when Angelina was born and insisted that she be made the baby's godmother, a request that her bemused parents eventually agreed to. Sarah may have wanted a formal responsibility for her sister because the idea of her beloved baby sister growing up to have slaves and ill-treating them was intolerable to her. She said, of her decision, many years later, 'I prayed that God would make me worthy of the task I had assumed and help me to guide and direct my precious child.' Angelina certainly felt the maternal influence of her elder sister throughout her life and often referred to her as 'mother'.

After their father died Sarah moved to Philadelphia in 1821 to become part of the Quaker community, leaving her Episcopalian roots behind. She converted her sister, convincing her to tear up her novels and wear plain clothes, but it was some years before both sisters became active opponents of slavery. They opposed slavery on moral and religious grounds, relying heavily on each other's support in the face of their friends and family's opposition. Angelina expressed their bond in a letter to her sister:

> *Thou art, dearest, my best beloved, and often does my heart expand with gratitude to the Giver of all good for the gift of such a friend, who has been the helper of my joy and the lifter up of my hands when they were ready to hang down in hopeless despair.*

Initially their opinions were expressed privately but Angelina's letter to a fellow abolitionist was published in a newspaper,

causing scandal amongst the Quakers and the mild disapproval
of her sister. Although Sarah had shaped her sister's views,
Angelina outgrew her influence. At a time when women were
not meant to have political views let alone voice them publicly,
Angelina wrote *An Appeal to the Christian Women of the South*
in 1836, a moving argument against slavery, and had the pam-
phlets distributed across the South. The sisters were told that
they would no longer be welcome in South Carolina.

They were, however, welcomed into the American Anti-
Slavery Association and started speaking in public in Boston,
firstly to groups of women only (the first time that any woman
had addressed a public gathering) but then also to men, many
of whom turned up uninvited and refused to go away. They
attracted audiences of a thousand, speaking from the heart
about their experiences of slavery and their belief that it was
profoundly wrong. Angelina became the first woman to give

evidence to a legislative body when she was asked to testify on slavery at the Massachusetts State Legislature. Sarah extended her campaigning to include women's rights; in her *Letters on the Equality of the Sexes and the Condition of Women* in 1838 she wrote:

> ... men and women were CREATED EQUAL ... Whatever is right for a man to do, is right for woman ... I seek no favors for my sex. I surrender not our claim to equality. All I ask of our brethren is that they will take their feet from off our necks and permit us to stand upright on that ground which God destined us to occupy.

Their mother was later to ask how she had managed to have such 'alien daughters'. The sisters were far ahead of their time but managed to influence women like them who would otherwise never have questioned slavery or their own limited civil rights. When the sisters discovered that their brother had had children by one of his slaves and died, leaving them enslaved to his son, they acknowledged them as family and took them in. Even liberal Boston was surprised. Angelina married, but this did not separate the sisters, who lived together and remained close until Sarah died in 1873, with her sister by her bedside. Angelina wrote to a friend of her loss: 'Dear friend, you know what I have lost, not a sister only, but a mother, friend, counsellor – everything I could lose in a woman.'

In British history the Pankhurst sisters are synonymous with votes for women but while they were devoted to their cause they fell out over how to achieve their aims. Their mother Emmeline, herself the child of politically active parents,

founded the Women's Social and Political Union (WSPU) in
1903, a women-only organisation to promote women's suffrage. Out of her three daughters, Christabel, Sylvia and Adela,
it was the eldest, Christabel, who was their mother's favourite,
being acknowledged as politically brilliant and the natural heir
to lead the suffragette movement. Christabel was charismatic
and media-savvy. Their mother's favouritism undoubtedly
caused some rivalry and bad feeling between the sisters. Sylvia
was artistic and emotional and Adela was less robust than her
sisters. The three young women all became involved in the
WSPU, which was dedicated to getting women the vote using
direct action such as demonstrating in front of parliament
(which led to Adela and Sylvia's arrest). Christabel was
arrested for spitting at a policeman. The WSPU stepped up its
action to include rallies, destroying property and advocating
hunger strikes by members once they were imprisoned. As
often happens with political movements, factions developed,
but in this case they involved members of a family. Sylvia was
fundamentally a socialist who did not feel happy with the
exclusion of men from the struggle for women's suffrage. She
set up her own east London federation of the suffragettes, initially with her mother's blessing, but when she aligned it to a
socialist group called the Herald League her mother and sister
expelled her from the WSPU. This was rough treatment
enough, but Mrs Pankhurst and Christabel were even more
brutal to poor Adela, whom they pushed into moving to
Australia in case she was influenced by Sylvia. Adela had been
depressed in her mid-twenties and was emotionally fragile.
The sisters were now on course for political divergence; Adela,
in a move not unrelated to her family's expulsion of her,

became a founding member of the right-wing Australia First Movement. In the Second World War she supported Japan, much to the horror of the other Pankhursts.

Being expelled from the WSPU had soured relations between Sylvia and Christabel, but the First World War, which Sylvia opposed and Christabel and their mother supported, further estranged them. Even the first victory for the suffragettes, the vote for some women over thirty which was achieved in 1918, did not achieve a family rapprochement. In 1927 Sylvia had a son and was still not reconciled with her family. In her book *The Suffragette Movement* she was critical of Christabel, arguing that her sister ignored the need for wider social reforms and was too damning of men. Even more damning was her description of how Christabel expelled her from the WSPU, at a time when Sylvia was recovering

from a hunger strike. Afterwards, she said, 'Christabel said that sometimes we should meet, "not as suffragettes, but as sisters". To me the words seemed meaningless; we had no life apart from the movement.'

Sylvia's demolition of Christabel included accusing her of putting women at risk by encouraging them to break the law and risk imprisonment, and of supporting their mother blindly. The fallout was profound but not unexpected. Even so Adela in Australia was upset and furious and it cemented Christabel's distrust of her sister.

Christabel and Sylvia had no contact for almost forty years until 1953, when Sylvia had a heart attack and was not expected to recover. That year, on her seventy-first birthday she received a letter from Christabel, who was living in Santa Monica but had heard of her sister's illness. The letter is conciliatory and recounts childhood memories:

Sylvia dear,

This is your birthday and I am writing to wish you, with my love, many happy returns of the day.

I hear that you are not as well as usual and I hope that you are improving and feeling stronger in this spring and your birthday month.

Your mind often goes back, I know, as mine does, to those good years of our childhood, when we still had Father and mother & the home they made for us.

When I went through mother's papers in 1928, I found among them a letter that I wrote to you from Geneva, where I was when Father died, in which I said to you how happy we had been, especially in those final years of his life when he

*had not left us, as he sometimes had to do, when his time was
divided between London & Manchester.*

*We had wonderful parents for whom we can always be
thankful, whose memory is as vivid with us now as it has
ever been.*

*Your son must be a great joy & comfort to you & I am sure
that there is a beautiful bond between you and him.*

*Of course, you are doing everything possible to safeguard
your health.*

*The years are passing us by & what strange – & by us in
our childhood – unexpected events & conditions they have
brought and are bringing in the world.*

*I view the things that are happening all over the globe
with concern, but with strong, with invincible hope in the
final triumph of goodness & justice & of glory, surpassing
all human dreams.*

*God's in His heaven: all must & will be right with the
world,*

Again my birthday love,
Your sister,
Christabel

Richard Pankhurst, Sylvia's son, remembers that his mother
was surprised to get the letter but felt it was genuine and
answered it immediately. The sisters continued to write to each
other until the end of summer 1957 (Christabel died six
months later), but their letters largely discussed misrepresenta-
tions of suffragette history in various books published at that
time, although Christabel was also keen to get some family
papers that were in Sylvia's possession. 'There was never a

meeting of minds,' says Richard Pankhurst. 'They both stuck to the ideological differences that they had at the beginning.' The letters were polite and careful; in their old age the sisters wanted to preserve a relationship. In true sisterly fashion, after Christabel's death, Sylvia said that despite their having lived apart for so long, she still felt a sense of loss.

7

Sisters of Powerful Men

Sisters of powerful men respond very differently to their brothers' rise to power. Napoleon's favourite sister revelled in the spoils of her brother's victories, stamping her feet when he didn't give her enough land or titles. King Charles II's sister was his long-standing confidante, while Lenin's sisters devoted their lives to the revolutionary cause. Hitler's sister Paula was never a prominent member of the Nazi party and would have preferred to be anonymous both before and especially after his death. All of them adored their brothers and suffered as well as prospered in their wake.

Pauline Bonaparte's life was totally entwined with that of her brother. The Bonapartes had eight children; Napoleon was the second son and Pauline, also known as Marie-Paulette, the middle sister of three. She was six when she first saw her brother because he had left their home in Corsica for a career in the military before she was born. He was seventeen on his return, and she was, perhaps because her father had died, eager to hero-worship him. The need for a paternal influence was strongly felt but Napoleon, after this initial visit, was rarely home. Pauline became a young teenager who had little interest in learning but a strong inclination to flirt with men and have a good time. There was clearly a difference between her driven, ambitious brother and this frivolous but good-natured young woman. Napoleon, however, liked playing the wiser, older brother while his younger sister enjoyed shopping and trying to ruin her reputation. Pauline so clearly adored and was loyal to her brother that he found it hard to censure her behaviour seriously. But from her teenage years her personal life was configured by her brother to suit his political ambitions. She fell in love with a French commissioner who had helped advance Napoleon's career, but her brother opposed the match once the commissioner ceased to be useful. Pauline fell into what was to be a recurrent pattern whenever her wishes were thwarted. She openly despaired and became ill. Napoleon ignored her behaviour – he was too busy fighting the Austrians – but as soon as he could he found her a more suitable husband in the shape of a general, Victor Emmanuel Leclerc.

By this time Pauline was a notable beauty and her brother proudly called her 'Beautiful Princess'. He, who was not a notably attractive man (at least physically), basked in the reflected glory of having a stunning sibling. Pauline was pleased with her husband but marriage at the age of seventeen did not control her. She quickly had a flirtation with her brother's aide-de-camp, who was also romantically involved with her brother's wife, Josephine. The favourite sister and the wife did not get on. Pauline could see some of herself in Josephine, particularly her ability to attract men, a talent that most sisters disapprove of in their brothers' wives. Trying to dislodge Josephine from her brother's life became an enduring hobby for Pauline. Another hobby was embarrassing her brother by befriending a series of unsuitable attractive men. As Napoleon continued his rise to power he became exasperated at his sister's impropriety. He was keen to establish a moral order in France and did not find her attraction for actors and soldiers at all endearing. This may have influenced his decision to send her husband (and therefore Pauline) to try to establish order in San Domingo, a French colony in the West Indies. Pauline allegedly wailed, 'How can my brother be so hard-hearted, so wicked, as to send me into exile among savages and snakes?' In reality Napoleon was rather cavalier in his insistence that Pauline should accompany her husband. The island was rife with yellow fever and there was intense fighting with insurgents. Leclerc implored his wife to escape with some French civil servants, to which she replied imperiously, 'You can quit, all of you. You are not Bonaparte's sister.'

She returned to France with a dead, embalmed husband. Her brother was by now effectively the ruler of France, having made himself First Consul. He preferred a plain and sombre dress and lifestyle while his sister, on receipt of a generous allowance from her brother (who felt a tinge of guilt at his sister's ordeal in San Domingo), bought a gilded carriage and a magnificent house on one of the most fashionable streets in Paris. It wasn't long before Napoleon again used his sister to further his own interests, but even in doing what her brother wanted Pauline managed to annoy him. Her marriage to the

Italian prince Camillo Borghese was not meant to take place until she had finished her mourning period for Leclerc, but she went ahead anyway. Napoleon wrote to her rather coldly, 'Love your husband, make a happy household, and above all do not be wanton and capricious. You are twenty-four, you ought by now to be mature and sensible.'

Their relationship warmed again after Napoleon became emperor and he welcomed his younger sister back into the bosom of the Bonaparte family. So warm was the welcome that rumours started about the nature of the sibling relationship. The story was helped by a remark made by Pauline to one of her ladies-in-waiting, who had caught the eye of her brother. As part of her argument that you couldn't refuse the emperor anything, she told her lady-in-waiting: 'Were he to tell me that he desired me, I would forget I was his sister and reply: "Your Majesty, I am yours to command."' One suspects Pauline was having a laugh but the comment reverberated round the French court. Scholars have not found any evidence of an incestuous relationship.

Although she was avaricious when Napoleon was in power, Pauline was intensely loyal to him even when he lost everything. When he began to be defeated in his military campaigns she sold one of her most valuable necklaces and sent him the money. When he lost his final battle at Leipzig and was exiled to Elba she offered to accompany him. 'I did not love the Emperor as a sovereign, but I loved him as a brother,' she said. She did indeed go to stay with him in Elba, until he escaped. When he was then imprisoned by the English on the island of St Helena Pauline pleaded to be able to see him and wrote passionately to the British prime minister asking him to move her brother to a warmer climate or else take responsibility for his death. She swore she would try to save him, and did her best, but Napoleon's health rapidly declined. Pauline never saw her brother again and vowed never to let an Englishman into her house as long as she lived.

There are similarities between the British king Charles II's sister Minette and Pauline, but only superficially. Minette was also strikingly beautiful, enjoyed parties and had affairs, but she had a serious, responsible side that made her Charles's closest confidante. Their letters are completely different from those of Napoleon and his younger sister; they discuss matters of state and political intrigues, although there is also some gossip and chat about fashion. Minette first met her brother in 1645 when she was fourteen months old and he was fourteen years old. The civil war had made it impossible for the royal family to stay together, although Minette was reunited with her mother and Charles in Paris before she was four. Like Pauline, she too was fatherless, as Charles I was executed when she was only six years old. Minette remained in France while her brother tried to restore the British monarchy, succeeding and becoming King Charles II. Minette rapidly became a favourite in the French court, with people lavishly praising her ability to please, her grace and her charm. These qualities ensured a good match for her, to no less a person than King Louis XIV's brother Philippe, who unfortunately turned out to be bisexual and in the thrall of a conniving aristocrat, the Chevalier de Lorraine. The marriage was also damaged early on by Louis himself, who had an affair with his new sister-in-law. The affair, though intense, did not last long but it made Philippe furious and bitterly jealous, to the extent that it coloured the relationship with his wife for ever. Louis, however, remained profoundly fond of Minette and spoke of his love for her throughout his life.

Minette was therefore in the unique position of being loved and trusted by two kings, who often had delicate matters of state to negotiate between them. How better to do that than through Minette, who was intelligent and discreet and genuinely had the wellbeing of both men and of both England (where she was born) and France (where she lived) at heart? Charles had envoys but they were never as successful as Minette at diplomacy.

Charles's relationship with his Minette was close and he was always solicitous of her health. In 1661 Charles wrote to her on hearing she was pregnant and feeling ill:

> *I have been in very much paine for your indisposition, not so much that I thought it dangerous, but for fear that you should miscarry. I hope now that you are out of that fear too, and for God's sake, my dearest sister have a care of yourselfe, and believe that I am more concerned for your health than I am in my owne, which I hope you do me that justice to be confident of, since you know how much I love you.*

The two definitely exchanged confidences. Minette must have told her brother that her husband was an inadequate lover, because he wrote to express his hope that he would be a better lover to his wife on their first night than Philippe had been to Minette.

Charles was always interested in his sister's opinion and trusted her with his own affairs of state. In a congratulatory letter to his sister on the birth of a son, he spends four lines on pleasantries and the rest telling her his dealings with the East India Company, which he hated. Less than a month after she had given birth he relied on her to negotiate with France when England looked in danger of going to war with Holland. If that had happened, France, due to a treaty in 1662, would have been obliged to defend Holland.

Minette pushed the English cause and found Louis keen to have an amicable agreement with England, only it had to be done secretly so as not to annoy the Dutch. But the relationship between the Dutch and English deteriorated so rapidly, with stories of atrocities on both sides, that war was inevitable.

Charles feared that Minette would be harmed by this and that he would no longer be able to write to her. But it seems that Louis had no real desire to be Charles's enemy either and peace was concluded quite swiftly.

Minette continued to intercede between her brother and brother-in-law and met her brother in Dover with terms of a new secret treaty. When it came to saying goodbye the strength of their feeling for each other was obvious to everyone. Charles, rather unregally, went back to hug his sister at least three times. One of the French noblemen present wrote to Louis saying that he had not realised how much two royal people could love each other. Minette, he felt, had more power over Charles than anyone else in the world.

Her mission accomplished, Minette returned to a life of intrigue with her husband, who had grown to hate her through her closeness to his brother, his own exclusion from matters of state and the influence of his own lovers. Louis had banished the Chevalier de Lorraine from court and Philippe blamed Minette. The death of Minette was sudden and shocking. At home with her husband she asked for her usual evening cup of chicory water and on drinking it screamed and rolled around with terrible pains in her stomach. She was convinced she had been poisoned and said so. But, concerned about the effect of her death and its inevitable rumours on her brother, she spoke to one of the people she could trust, imploring them not to tell Charles. 'Spare him the grief at all events and do not let him take revenge on the king here for he is at least not guilty.' She asked for a ring of hers to be given to her brother and died, in great discomfort, eight hours after drinking the chicory water.

Louis ordered a post-mortem but the doctors did not agree on its findings, which were that she had died of cholera morbus, a non-specific diagnosis once applied to stomach inflammations with vomiting and stomach cramps.

When Charles heard he was devastated, railing at Minette's husband for being a 'villain'. He was convinced she had been poisoned and shut himself away for five days, too overwhelmed with grief to see anyone. In France it was believed that Philippe's lover, the Chevalier de Lorraine, and some of his friends had poisoned Minette, but without the knowledge of her husband. Charles, aware of how much the Treaty of Dover had meant to his sister, remembered her wise words and decided not to break off relations with France by accusing members of its royal family of murdering Minette.

The sisters of Vladimir Ilich Lenin – born Ulyanov – had their own wise words but it is debatable how receptive their brother was to hearing them. There were initially eight Ulyanovs but two children died at birth. The eldest of the children, Anna, was devoted to Aleksandr, the eldest boy, and in her writings about him she speaks of his maturity and thoughtfulness. That she idolised him is clear and it is likely that the others, including Vladimir, did too. To understand the devotion to the Russian revolutionary cause of Anna and two of her sisters, one need look no further than to the execution of this beloved brother. Aleksandr was arrested for his part in a plot to assassinate the tsar, and between his arrest and execution he was not allowed to see his family. Anna wrote to him in despair as his execution date approached. 'There is no one better on earth or more kindly than you. It's not just me who'll say this, as a sister: everyone who knew you will say this, my beloved little sun!' Her brother wrote back wishing her every happiness and saying farewell. It was a terrible tragedy for Anna and she did not fill his empty pedestal with Vladimir, who she felt was arrogant and rude. Her sister Maria, however, did elevate Vladimir to a more special place in her affections and she was close to him throughout their lives. She described her relationship with the leader of the Russian revolution as follows: 'I had a sort of absolutely special feeling towards Vladimir Ilich: warm love together with a form of worship . . . He never showed any strictness to me, even the other way round, he spoiled me, as the youngest of the family.' The two lived together for much of their adult life.

The sister nearest Vladimir in age was Olga, and the two played together as they were growing up. All three girls, unusually for the time, were given the same education that their brothers had. All did outstandingly well, Anna and Olga graduating with gold medals. Anna had once been told by Aleksandr that her biggest fault was that she lacked social convictions; perhaps in comparison to him, she did. But Aleksandr's death did revolutionise his siblings. Vladimir and Anna were forced into exile, and Olga threatened to kill the tsar herself. The two exiles read and talked a lot about political theory together, although this was risky: they were watched by the police because they were considered dangerous influences on those around them.

Olga died tragically young at the age of twenty, of typhoid fever, but she had already made some useful revolutionary connections that her brother used when he was allowed to return to St Petersburg. Maria was slower to be recruited to the revolutionary cause but she started the meetings her siblings held at the family house. Vladimir spent time with his favourite sister working on her revolutionary education and telling her what she should read. Maria was easily influenced by her brother. Even when he moved away, he wrote to her asking for updates about what she was reading.

Anna risked her life for her brother and the cause, raising money, establishing safe houses and publishing propaganda. When her brother was imprisoned, Anna and the family moved to be near the prison and Anna provided not only supplies but also political updates. They spoke in code on her visits; their talk of family get-togethers and musical events hid details of the size of public demonstrations and the number of arrests. Their correspondence contained tiny dots and dashes within letters that to Vladimir and his sister conveyed priceless information; in this way Vladimir produced a whole political programme for a forthcoming meeting. This system continued after Vladimir was sent to Siberia. Anna travelled abroad to gather support for her brother's cause, while Maria joined the Moscow underground movement. Maria was arrested and at one stage was in solitary confinement for seven months, during which time her brother wrote continually to her. Other brothers might have written sympathetic letters; Vladimir sent pragmatic tips for how to cope, by alternating reading with translating and saving fiction for the evening.

When Vladimir returned from exile in Europe in 1917 after the fall of Tsar Nicholas II, he stayed with his sisters for three months. He became worried by Maria's workload, urging her to go away to get medical treatment for her legs and nerves which were bothering her. Rather sweetly he told her that although these were troubled times nothing much was going on. However much he loved his cause, Vladimir cared for and wanted to protect his sister.

In 1917 Vladimir was elected chair of the Council of People's Commissars by the Russian Congress of Soviets. He was living with his wife and Maria, and Anna was close by. They all worked together, now openly, on the future of the Soviet Union. Maria did what many sisters do and argued with her sister-in-law, sometimes about housework and mostly about the poor diet Vladimir was eating. Anna and Vladimir spoke every day on the phone, with Anna working to provide care for orphaned and homeless children.

After Vladimir survived an assassination attempt and a series of strokes that left him incapacitated, Maria, keen to ensure it wasn't just his wife looking after him, jointly assumed responsibility for his nursing care. Anna visited frequently. Maria, despite her devotion to her brother, politically leaned towards Stalin and often thought he was right. She tried to shelter Vladimir from current affairs and rowed with her sister-in-law over what was best for her brother. She wanted him to be left in peace; his wife wanted him to continue at the heart of Soviet politics. Maria herself could not stop her involvement in politics and after Lenin died in 1924 she felt compelled to keep his memory and vision alive. She warned Stalin of the dangers of individual leaders and reminded him that Lenin had said only collective work could provide the right leadership of the party. This unsurprisingly contributed to her fall from favour in the Party. Anna, too, virtually retired from political life in the mid-1920s, writing to Maria that she was bored but worried that Maria was still working too hard. Her letters contain a mix of self-pity, envy and genuine concern:

I do nothing. In the morning we stroll, after lunch sleep; then we stroll till dinner and see, now at ten, I write to you by the light of a candle end and it's soon, again to bed. Try a little of such a regime my dear! Or your older sister will be ashamed to arrive in good health, while you are pale and exhausted.

Her letters to Maria were full of advice on how she should look after herself; she was urged to marvel at nature as Vladimir had done and to be more philosophical.

Anna, however, was setting herself up for a collision with Stalin by arguing over how her brother would be represented in his biography. Anna was keen to publicise Vladimir's Jewish roots, in an attempt to reduce anti-Semitism, but Stalin repeatedly refused. Both sisters were constantly asked for help in critiquing biographies of their brother and to supply letters and other papers. They devoted themselves to writing to biographers pointing out inaccuracies. Both sisters were celebrated, the more so after Stalin's reign was over, but when Anna died in 1935 she was given a state funeral, as was Maria when she died two years afterwards. Maria's obituary spoke of her devotion to her brother: how she took care of his food, clothes and everything else, so that he never had to think about trivia. In fact although their relationship to Vladimir was profound, both sisters were revolutionaries in their own right.

It used to overawe people to meet Lenin's sisters. Yet to meet the sister of the most infamous tyrant in modern history was perhaps even more extraordinary. The American army officer who interviewed Hitler's sister Paula in June 1945 was struck by the family resemblance. 'The likeness to her brother in appearance, look and physiognomy is striking and intensifies the longer one is in her presence.'

Paula was the younger sister of Adolf Hitler and the only one of his full siblings (he did have other half-siblings) to live through childhood. Their parents, Alois and his third wife Klara, lived in Austria and, like all the other sisters in this chapter, Paula lost her father when she was young, at the age of six. Paula said in her interview that she spent little time with her brother, who was seven years older than her, and that he was regularly hit by their father (whom she describes as a conservative old Austrian official) for staying out late and generally being disobedient. Their mother was more lenient and affectionate. The children did not mind losing their father, who collapsed over his morning pint of beer in the local bar, but when their mother died nearly five years later they were devastated. Paula's account of her brother is of a young man who loved music, history and painting but came home with terrible school reports.

After his mother's death Adolf moved to Vienna and Paula was looked after by her aunt. Adolf sent her advice and books to read to improve herself. 'Naturally he was the great brother for me, but I submitted to his authority only with inner resistance. In fact we were brother and sister, who did frequently quarrel, but were fond of each other and yet often spoiled each other's pleasure of living together.' Should one be surprised that Adolf Hitler could behave like a concerned brother? Paula saw her brother infrequently during his rise to power although his political activity had a direct effect on her; she was fired from her secretarial job in Vienna when it became known she was a relative of Adolf's and she decided to change her name to Wolf.

Paula's account of her relationship with her brother, as told to the American general who interviewed her, is that it was distant. She said she met Adolf only once a year through the 1930s until 1941, although he paid her an allowance. She attended one of the Nuremberg rallies but claimed she had never been a member of the Nazi Party. In a memorable understatement she said, 'I must honestly confess that I would have preferred it if he had followed his original ambition and become an architect. It would have saved the world a lot of troubles.' She never openly admitted that she knew the full horror of what her brother had done and is likely to have been much more sympathetic to his fascist beliefs than she was willing to confess to the Americans. But she didn't hide her emotion at Adolf's death. She sobbed to her interrogator: 'The personal fate of my brother affected me very much, He was still my brother, no matter what happened. His end brought unspeakable sorrow to me, as his sister.'

8

Multiple Sisters

If having one sister is proof that you're not unique then what happens when you have more than one? With a choice of sisters you may find one you're more likely to get on with. On the other hand it may be harder to assert yourself, to be an individual, when there are two or more girls just like you running around. In some families an abundance of sisters seems to spur each sister on to greater heights, to outdo each other. Certainly some of the sisters here led remarkable lives and were clearly influenced (sometimes ill-advisedly) by each other. Sometimes the effect of having more than one sister was supportive and liberating, in other families it created jealousies and twarted aspirations. Even in the sunniest stories of sisters there are shadows.

If any story idolises sisterhood it is *Little Women*, the American childhood classic that tells of the trials of the March sisters, Meg, Jo, Beth and Amy. The author, Louisa May Alcott, drew heavily on her own three sisters to tell how the March girls coped with their father being away at war and overcame constant poverty and childish selfishness to grow into well-rounded women. *Little Women*, however, is more than a story of defeating adversity through sisterly teamwork. It is a description of the attempts of Jo (a thinly disguised Louisa) to be the calm 'little woman' that her father wants her to be. When Jo cries bitterly to her mother, 'It seems as if I could do anything when I am in a passion; I get so savage, I could hurt any-one, and enjoy it,' this is Louisa's own anguish at being unable to control her passions. *Little Women* was partly an attempt to appease her father, a portrait of the family and daughter she knew he wanted to have.

The Alcotts were not a traditional nineteenth-century American family. Amos Brown Alcott set up an experimental school which failed, following which the family tried commu-nity living and then surviving on handouts. They moved around so much that the girls relied on each other for friend-ship. Anna, the eldest sister, was pretty and placid and her

father's clear favourite, whereas poor Louisa was such an unsettled baby that her parents both said she made them unhappy. Anna was capable of slyly whack-ing her sister when she thought no one was look-ing. But by the time Louisa was three it was she who was hit-ting her elder sister. Amos wrote in his journals describing the girls' devel-opment that 'Anna suffers a good deal from this temper of her sister's. She bears the mark of her sister's hand, at pres-ent, on her cheek.' Louisa's tantrums were blown out of all proportion by her lofty-minded parents. 'Louisa gave signs of impending evil yesterday,' wrote her father.

Louisa constantly compared her father's close relationship with her sister to the coolness with which he treated her. But the girls were close. When Amos went on a trip with Anna in search of a new community Louisa wrote a poem mourning her sister's absence.

> Sister, dear, when you are lonely,
> Longing for your distant home,
> And the images of loved ones
> Warmly to your heart shall come.
> Then, mid tender thoughts and fancies,
> Let one fond voice say to thee,
> 'Ever when your heart is heavy,
> Anna, dear, then think of me.'

Anna took an unusually long time to get married, finally leaving home at twenty-nine, but Louisa still felt abandoned when she left. In *Little Women* Louisa modelled Meg on Anna, and whether she meant to make her so or not, Meg is plainly dull, the wife of a decent man, whose only vice is to want a decent pair of gloves. The Beth of *Little Women*, the uncomplaining, much-loved sister, is Louisa's second sister Lizzie, and the frivolous Amy her youngest sister May. Lizzie, like Beth, caught scarlet fever after visiting poor families in the neighbourhood. She never fully recovered and over the next two years lost weight and became frail and fretful. Lizzie, like Beth March, had a little bell she would ring when she needed something. It was usually Louisa and her mother who ran to her, and they who nursed her as she become skeletal and racked with pain. From the end of 1857 until Lizzie's death in the following March Louisa devoted herself to her invalid sister, but it was a horrible time. Lizzie became uncomfortable sitting downstairs and Louisa would sit beside her for hours in her bedroom, knowing that otherwise Lizzie would have nothing to eat or drink because she would not want to trouble anyone, talking to her while she sewed. It was when Lizzie whispered that her needle was too heavy that the sisters sensed she was close to death.

In a letter to her cousin, Louisa describes the death of Lizzie at the age of twenty-three.

> *Last Friday night after suffering much of the day, she asked to lie in father's arms & called us all about her holding our hands & smiling at us as she silently seemed to bid us goodbye . . . At midnight she said 'Now I'm comfortable & so happy,' & soon after became unconscious. We sat beside her while she quietly breathed her life away, opening her eyes to give us one beautiful look before they closed forever.*

Not only was the house empty without her but Lizzie's death deprived Louisa of her role as the most needed sister.

Louisa had an ambivalent relationship with May, whose ability to get what she wanted left Louisa in a state of bemused pride and resentment. In *Little Women* it is Amy who gets the trip to Europe, the rich husband, the lovely clothes. In real life May's art lessons in Europe were paid for by Louisa (although the two sisters also travelled together to Europe). May married happily, but died prematurely in childbirth. Her daughter, named Louisa, which reflects May's attachment to her sister, was shipped from Europe to America for Aunt Louisa to bring up.

When *Little Women* was published in 1868 it sold so well that her publishers asked Louisa to produce a series of books based on the March family, and she wrote *Good Wives*, *Little Men* and then *Jo's Boys*. She never married, and although her little niece called her 'Mother' and the two adored each other, Louisa struggled to look after her as she had developed symptoms of mercury poisoning, a result of treatment for typhoid fever when she was thirty. Louisa died two days after her father, at the age of fifty-six, without her sister beside her. Anna wrote: 'Just how life is to be lived without the dearest companion who for more than fifty years has been nearest and dearest to my heart I do not yet see.'

The Alcotts were a set of poor sisters; the Jeromes were much richer. The fortunes of the Jerome sisters were inter-related, and although Jennie Jerome is known best as the mother of Winston Churchill, there is more to the sisters than producing one extraordinary man. There were originally four girls, Clara, Jennie, Camille and Leonie, but Camille died from a fever at the age of seven. The girls were brought up to be as marriageable as possible, with the understanding that their rich husbands were likely to stray and it was their job to look beautiful, be dignified and put up with it.

The family travelled round Europe, and Jennie, who was an acknowledged beauty, fell in love almost at first sight with Randolph Churchill, the second son of the seventh Duke of Marlborough. Despite the lack of enthusiasm (the Jeromes were after first sons) the marriage went ahead and Jennie's sisters were thus also catapulted into the British aristocracy. They did their best to support each other. Jennie confided in Leonie when Randolph became mentally ill with syphilis. His brain was sufficiently damaged for him to have to resign his post as Chancellor of the Exchequer. As he became seriously ill he insisted that Jennie accompany him on a rather nightmarish last-gasp cruise. Jennie wrote to Leonie about how terrible it was to be cruising with a husband who was half out of his mind. But with characteristic pride she warned Leonie that she did not require sisterly intervention. 'Pity or mere sympathy even from you is wasted on me,' she wrote.

After Clara, the oldest sister, died, the Duke of Connaught (a friend of Clara's) wrote to Leonie's sister-in-law, describing rather sentimentally the sisters' bond. 'It was indeed a beautiful affection – strong and deeply sympathetic – that weathered for eighty years life's misfortunes as well as its joys and united these three sisters, so different, yet so attached, with a bond broken only by death.'

Perhaps more has been written about the Mitfords than about any other sisters in recent history but it is impossible to write about sisters without a mention of them. When Deborah, the youngest Mitford sister, was asked who was in her family she replied, 'Three giants, three dwarves and one brute.' The 'giants' were her elder sisters, Nancy, Pamela and Diana. The 'dwarves' were Unity, Jessica and herself; the 'brute' her only brother Tom. This English aristocratic family became famous for the scandalous behaviour of some of the six daughters as well as for their achievements: Nancy and Jessica became writers and Deborah married the Duke of Devonshire and preserved Chatsworth House as a magnificent stately home.

Each of them was shaped by the intense love, rivalry, selflessness and flashes of hatred that characterise many sisterly relationships. Without each other's influence, they might have grown up very differently. Their feelings for each other were later polarised by their extreme political views; on the one side were Diana and Unity, passionate supporters of Hitler, and on the other was Jessica, an equally committed communist. It was controversially said by Peter Rudd, Nancy's husband, that Jessica only became a communist to get even with Unity. The others' political views fell somewhere in between, although mostly to the right.

Nancy and Jessica used their lives as material in their books and almost all the sisters, in various interviews, spoke colourfully about their relationships with each other. But most of all they wrote to each other: in total, around twelve thousand letters.

The sisters fell into two camps initially because of their ages. There was almost a generation between the oldest and youngest; Nancy was fifteen when Deborah was born. Their parents subscribed to the philosophy of bringing up children by affectionate neglect, denying them conventional schooling while encouraging them to read *The Times*. The sisters spent their time together, making up their own language, 'Boudledidge', and nicknames, and both playing with and tormenting each other. The girls' views on sisters varied from Nancy's belief that they protected you from 'life's cruel circumstances' to Jessica's retort that they *were* 'life's cruel circumstances'.

Nancy, as the eldest, was the most affected by the arrival of sisters. She was three when Pamela was born and said later that it 'threw me into a permanent rage for about twenty years'. Tom and then Diana followed quite quickly but Nancy was meanest to Pamela. It was Diana, however, who was Nancy's main rival; her beauty and brains meant that she always understood and attracted men. Nancy was jealous of Diana for her entire life.

Deborah seems to have been the most immune from Nancy's spiteful tongue. She always said that she adored Nancy and as the youngest, she may have been the most sisterly sister. In a letter to Diana in 1965 she wrote, 'Wouldn't it be dread if one had a) no sisters b) sisters who didn't write.'

As the three elder sisters moved into society, the younger ones watched enviously. Pamela was the first to get engaged and married, to a rich scientist, Derek Jackson, although they later divorced. It was Diana who made the most glamorous marriage, to Bryan Guinness, an heir and the catch of the season. Their married life was short-lived; Diana met Oswald Mosley in 1932 at a dinner party and although she wasn't the first woman to be mesmerised by his charm, the passion was mutual. Mosley had been a member of parliament but was about to form the British Union of Fascists. Diana, despite her two sons, began an affair with him and left her husband. Even her parents were forced to take notice; they forbade the younger sisters to visit Diana. Nancy, however, supported her, perhaps secretly pleased that the family's golden girl had tripped off her pedestal, although she did sound a word of caution when she wrote to her:

> *Darling I do hope you are making a right decision. You are SO young to begin getting it wrong in the world, if that's what's going to happen.*
>
> *However, it is all your own affair & whatever happens I shall always be on your side as you know & so will anybody who cares for you & perhaps the rest don't really matter.*

To which Diana replied, 'You are divine to me, I don't know what I would do without you.'

Diana's passion for the man became a passion for his politics. In 1933 she went to Germany, to gather support for her husband, and attended the first Nuremberg rally. She took Unity with her, the sister least equipped to resist the lure of a fanatical cause. Both of them came away obsessed with Hitler. It was the beginning of the political chasm between the sisters that became permanent.

The three younger sisters had grown up quite apart from their elder sisters. Unity, known as Boud, was the least articulate of the sisters and her disruptive behaviour prompted their mother to send her to various boarding schools, all of which asked her to leave. Jessica adopted socialist principles early on, deciding that it was unfair for them to be so rich when others were living in poverty. Deborah (Debo), pretty and good-natured, generally caused little trouble at all. Jessica's memoir *Hons and Rebels* and Nancy's novel *The Pursuit of Love* recount their childhood in completely different ways. Nancy's childhood is fictionalised as fun and whimsical; Jessica's is restricted to the point of suffocation. Jessica's description of her sisters, then unmarried, is beautifully observed:

> Boud, Debo and I were too uncomfortably close in age for friendship. We got in each other's way dreadfully in the fierce and competitive struggle to grow up. Boud, three years older than I, hated being classified with me and Debo as 'the little ones'; I in turn tearfully resented being lumped with Debo, two years my junior, as 'the Babies'. Nancy was too sharp-tongued and sarcastic to be anyone's favourite sister for long. She might suddenly turn her penetrating emerald eyes in one's direction and say, 'Run along up to the schoolroom, we've all had quite enough of you,' or, if one had taken particular trouble to do one's hair in ringlets, she was apt to remark, 'You look like the oldest and ugliest of the Brontë sisters today.' Pam, now that she had abandoned hope of becoming a horse, was too stolidly immersed in country life, devoid of the restless unformu-lated longing for change that, in one way or another, gripped the rest of us. But Diana had the necessary quali-ties for a favourite sister. She was bored and rebellious, all right, a follower in Nancy's footsteps. If not an initiator of jokes, she was at least a roarer at them, and inclined to take an interest in me.

Mosley's wife had died, and he and Diana married in a cere-mony which took place in Goebbels's house, attended by

Hitler. This marriage, as well as her undying loyalty to fascism, estranged her from Jessica. Jessica never forgave her and destroyed all but one of Diana's letters. They only met again when Nancy was dying, although Diana wrote of her desire to be friends with her sister and Jessica was surprised to find she still felt love for Diana when she saw her.

In comparison Jessica did not cut Unity, who was now deep in one-sided love for Hitler, out of her life. Their letters are some of the most genuinely warm and affectionate of all of the Mitford sisters' correspondence. They read like two sisters having a chat. Unity, who wrote to a German newspaper announcing she was proud to be a Jew-hater, was the embodiment of everything that Jessica detested. Yet Jessica said, 'I love my Boud in spite of it all.'

When Jessica eloped, much to her family's distress, with her cousin Esmond Romilly, who was also a communist, Unity wrote to tell Jessica that she loved her and would try to be friends with Esmond although if she had to shoot him for her cause she would do so. Tragically, when Britain declared war on Germany, Unity's response was to shoot herself in the head. She returned to England to be nursed by her mother, but was reduced to a pitiful, childlike state, dying of meningitis in 1948. Until her death Jessica would lie to her husband and visit her.

Meanwhile Nancy was about to do something that would, when it came out, destroy Diana's feelings for her. In 1940 Oswald Mosley was imprisoned as a threat to national security. Nancy was called to the Home Office to give information about Diana. Nancy did not hold back. She advised the Home Office to look at how often Diana had been to Germany and said: 'I regard her as an extremely dangerous person.' Diana was taken away from her eleven-week-old baby and put into Holloway Prison; she was imprisoned for over three years. 'Not very sisterly behaviour', said Nancy flippantly of herself. Many people would say Diana deserved it and that Nancy did her duty; perhaps, then, it is unfair to read other motives into her behaviour, such as a desire to get even with a sister who had always had everything (including four children, while Nancy was unable to have any).

Nancy went out of her way to support Diana once she had helped to incarcerate her. She wrote letters and had Diana's older boys to stay when they visited their mother. It wasn't until after Nancy's death that Diana learnt of her sister's submission to the Home Office. She said that Nancy was the most disloyal person she had ever known.

When Jessica's memoir was published in 1960, it was with some trepidation that she sent a copy to Nancy, the established writer of the family. As usual Nancy couldn't resist a small swipe at a sister. 'A slightly cold wind to the heart perhaps – you don't seem very fond of anybody . . .' Deborah liked it, but Diana was cross at being depicted as a dumb society beauty.

All sisterly estrangements were momentarily suspended when Nancy, who had moved to France, became ill with cancer. Diana, who lived nearby, visited her frequently, but Nancy got the most comfort from Pamela, who was unobtrusive but soothing. Deborah wrote constantly and Jessica, who lived in America, visited three times. The old patterns of sisterly behaviour reasserted themselves as Nancy, racked with pain, would be critical of whatever was done for her. On one occasion she asked Jessica to bring up some roses from the garden, only to snap at her, 'I can't think why you didn't get them earlier, you've nothing else to do.'

It was Deborah who wrote to Jessica to tell her that Nancy had died. Deborah reflected, 'I know she had success as a writer but what is that compared to things like proper husbands & lovers & children – think of all the loneliness of all these years, so sad.' The loss of Nancy prompted Diana to write to Jessica, a sweet letter, describing the funeral. Diana wrote one more letter to Jessica, years later, when she heard her sister was dying, but this has been lost.

Diana was unhappy that Pamela and Deborah continued to be friends with Jessica; she said that she would have struggled to stay in touch with someone who had been so beastly to either of them. But, showing the compassion that siblings so often retain, Jessica could still feel for Diana. When Mosley died she wrote a short letter to Deborah asking in a roundabout way for her to pass on her condolences.

Pamela died, followed by Jessica, leaving Deborah and Diana. Deborah wrote or faxed to her remaining sister almost every day, the written communication continuing because Diana was too deaf to talk to on the telephone. When Diana died in France in the summer of July 2003 there were no more sisterly letters to write.

The Andrews sisters didn't write many letters to each other but that's because they could never get away from each other. They sang together and spent almost every minute of every day together but despite being the first global girl band they did not have much in common. LaVerne, Maxene and Patty, from Minneapolis, sang close harmony (Patty, the youngest, was the lead singer), specialising in boogie-woogie and swing. They started their professional career touring with a big band in the 1930s and went on to sell over seventy-five million records, have forty-six top ten hits and make numerous Hollywood films.

Their hectic schedule meant that they did little else but practise, perform, eat and sleep. Their parents were so heavily involved with their act that when they died it was inevitably disruptive. By the early 1950s Patty had married the group's piano player, who took on a more managerial position and started arguing that she deserved a higher salary than her sisters because she was the lead vocalist. Her elder sisters were appalled as they had always split the money equally on the basis they all worked as hard as each other. When Patty announced she was setting up a solo career, it was how she did it that really rankled. The sisters found out by reading it in a newspaper.

Maxene and LaVerne, who continued to work together, were, however, still understanding about the split. Maxene was quoted as saying that 'we were as different as day and night. The only thing we really had in common – outside the love of our parents – was the love of our work. We didn't like each other's boyfriends, we didn't like each other's taste in clothes, and so there was always little sparks there.'

When LaVerne and Maxene went on a television show and did a sketch in which the host dressed up as Patty, their youngest sister had a sense of humour failure and instructed her lawyers. Patty then declared war by taking LaVerne to court over the distribution of their late parents' assets. The sisters would not even look at each other in court.

Show business, however, prevailed. Within two years the sisters forgave and forgot and returned to working together until LaVerne died in 1967. It took nearly a decade for the remaining Andrews sisters to fall out, this time over contract negotiations. The sisters each had their own representation and this time they were estranged for good. Patty refused to talk to Maxene, and despite Maxene trying publicly for reconciliation the sisters never got over their rift. Patty said that Maxene had been jealous of her, but what little sister doesn't say that? Maxene once said that she wouldn't have changed her life for anything, but 'I would wish I had the ability and the power to bridge the gap between my relationship with my sister Patty. I haven't found the way yet, but I'm sure that the Lord will find the way.' Maxene died before any way was found.

Alice O'Keeffe on her sisters

Secretly, I feel very sorry for people who don't have sisters. I'm the eldest of four, all girls. My mother says we always got on well growing up and didn't really scrap, probably because we were quite evenly spaced – four years between me and the next eldest, and then a three-year gap between each of the others. During my childhood it meant there was always a baby in the house, a real-life doll to cuddle and parade around with in the school playground. It meant there was always someone to play with – and for 'play with' read 'boss around'. And four is a lot; a gang, a force to be reckoned with.

People have always said that the family resemblance is strong. 'Are you so-and-so's sister?' is a question I used to get asked all the time, and am still likely to hear whenever I go home to the part of London where we grew up. My middle two sisters are often mistaken for each other: at M—'s engagement drinks one of her school friends rushed up to H— to offer congratulations only to be told, 'Um, you've got the wrong sister.'

But, for me, it was after a traumatic break-up in my thirties that the sisterly bond, always strong, was tempered to steel. My then boyfriend of ten years walked out and I fell apart. I stopped sleeping, stopped eating. It hurt to breathe. My sisters closed ranks around me with a fierce protectiveness. Long after friends had tired of hearing about it, and I had tired of talking about it, my sisters were there. It's a special kind of wordless comfort, to sit on the sofa and watch *EastEnders* with those you have known all their lives. There's nobody on your side more than your blood.

Having a sister is like having a built-in best friend. You can fall out but you know it won't last. One of my sisters now lives abroad but every time we see each other we pick up as though from the night before. It's a conversation that spans a lifetime, perhaps interrupted weeks at a time, but seemingly unaffected. My sisters are among the most fun people I know to just have a drink with, see a film, go on holiday. If we weren't related I think we would be good friends and I'm extraordinar-ily grateful for that.

It makes me very sad to hear of sis-ters who are estranged. Imagine the waste of having a sister you never speak to. I saw a film recently where two sisters had been separated when one was quite

young, and were only reunited as adults. Tears welled long before the emotional final scene. How unimaginably awful to be denied that relationship; to have a sister but not to know her.

I know I can ring any one of my sisters at any time of the day or night, she won't necessarily thank me but she will pick up. When a leaking boiler in my new flat panicked me at quarter to midnight I called my sister. Whether life-changing news or something totally inconsequential, I will often speak to my sister first. My sisters are there when I need them as I hope I am for them. Friends are wonderful, of course, but friendships can be outgrown and you can never outgrow a sister. She'll always be there, someone you've known your whole life. A shared childhood means a childhood never forgotten; there's always someone to ask, 'What was the name of that . . .?' or 'Do you remember when we . . .?' I'm so grateful to have my three sisters; when we are all together it's the best thing in the world.

9

Brothers and Sisters

'You don't notice brothers so much,' is the view of my youngest daughter, whose only brother is thirteen years older than she is. The age gap between them may make this distance inevitable but brothers and sisters often don't achieve the intimacy that sisters do with sisters. They may be even more competitive but it depends on what they're good at. Many of the sisters in this book had one or more brothers, with whom they had a less significant relationship than they did with a sister. The Brontës, Austens, Stephens and Mitfords had brothers, as did Queen Elizabeth I. They were all deeply fond of their brothers and the loss of them affected all of their lives but their world orbited more strongly round a sister. Sisters are more tied to their families than their brothers, more likely to be the ones to take responsibility for ageing parents and younger siblings. They are more likely to support each other as they grow older.

In different cultures brothers and sisters have clearly defined roles. Margaret Mead in the 1950s compared the American middle-class family which encouraged sibling competitiveness with the Samoan way of bringing up boys and girls separately to avoid interaction. There is a Hindu festival that celebrates the relationship between brothers and sisters, called Raksha Bandhan, in which a sister ties a thread on to the wrist of her elder brother, who promises to look after her. The elder sister then promises the same to her younger brother and the brothers and sisters feed each other sweets.

Historically brothers were by far the most important siblings. To be the oldest brother in the family was to be the one who inherited everything that mattered. Brothers were left in charge of their sisters when they became head of the family. Yet this didn't mean the relationship was never emotionally close. Although sisterhood has a poor showing in ancient times there are glimpses of sisters and brothers having warm and close relationships. In Menander's comedy *Dyskolos* ('The Misanthrope'), Gorgias deceives his stepfather so that his stepsister can make a decent marriage. His reason for this sibling loyalty? 'It isn't possible to escape a relationship with a sister.' For most of history only boys were routinely educated, while their sisters made do with whatever scraps of knowledge they passed on. Some sisters, like the de Beauvoirs, were only educated because they didn't have any brothers.

For much of history, too, just as talented wives contributed to their husbands' success behind the scenes, so sisters inspired and lent their creative talents to their brothers. Sometimes their lives were almost inseparable. The stories of Dorothy Wordsworth and Fanny Mendelssohn are two such examples. Mary Lamb's influence over her brother Charles's life and Fanny Dickens's effect on her brother Charles's writing illustrate the same point but in different ways.

Dorothy Wordsworth adored her brother William. Just how much and in what way she adored him have been speculated on for over two hundred years. What is clear, however, is her influence on his writing and her own ability to write prose of startling beauty in her journals. She was born in 1771, a year after William, into a family of four brothers whose childhood was shattered when first their mother and then their father died. Dorothy went to live with her mother's parents, who were mean-spirited and strict. When her brothers came home from boarding school it was William who understood her misery and comforted her. William's poem 'The Vale of Esthwaite' connects the love he has for Dorothy with the love he had for his mother:

> Sister for whom I feel a love
> That warms a brother far above,
> On you, as sad she marks the scene,
> Why does my heart so fondly lean?

Once William went to university Dorothy barely saw him but he wrote often, saying that whenever he saw a beautiful scene he wished she could see it too. For Dorothy this was intoxicating stuff. Unloved for most of her childhood, she was deeply touched by her clever brother's feelings for her. She wrote to a friend:

I am willing to allow that half the virtues with which I fancy him endowed are the creation of my own love; but

surely I may be excused! He was never tired of comforting his
sister; he never left her in anger; he always met her with joy;
he preferred her society to every other pleasure – or rather,
when we were so happy as to be within each other's reach, he
had no pleasure when we were compelled to be divided.

There was wish-fulfilment on both sides. When William
came to stay in Norfolk the two began walking together, locked
in intense discussions. To their joy they managed to get a
cottage in Dorset where they could live together on the understanding that they would be housekeepers for the absent
landlord. This move coincided with William going through a
period of depression. Dorothy devoted herself to raising his
spirits and encouraged his writing, offering kind but con-
structive criticism of his poetry. He described her restorative
influence on him in *The Prelude*:

> Companion never lost through many a league –
> Maintained for me a saving intercourse
> With my true self; for though bedimmed and changed
> Both as a cloud and a waning moon,
> She whispered still that brightness should return,
> She, in the midst of all, preserved me still
> A Poet, made me seek beneath that name,
> And that alone, my office upon earth.

Dorothy was more than a sister to William, she was his muse,
confidante and, more mundanely, his housekeeper. Her own
writing shows her talents of observation. Some of her prose is
beautiful, and her descriptions of nature are in places equal to
her brother's. But she would never have thought of herself as a

gifted writer. Her life was utterly subsumed in making her brother's life complete.

But by William's early thirties, his sister's love was not enough. He decided, after consulting with his sister, to get married. Dorothy, who had never wanted a husband, was privately distraught. The day he went to propose to Mary (a friend of them both), she wandered round their cottage and wrote in her journal, 'I will be busy; I will look & be well when he comes back to me. O, the Darling! Here is one of his bitten apples! I can hardly find it in my heart to throw it into the fire.'

William's marriage helped dispel the speculation amongst the literary community in London that he and Dorothy had an incestuous relationship. Some biographers have also suggested their love was sexual but there is no direct evidence of this other than William's demonstrative affection and emotional dependence on his sister and the fact they were both eccentric. But their relationship was unusually intense. The night before William's wedding Dorothy slept with the wedding ring on her finger, handing it over sadly the next morning. She described lying motionless on her bed as her brother and Mary said their vows. She recovered sufficiently to live with William and Mary, becoming a devoted aunt and sister-in-law. She fell ill in 1829 and Mary nursed her. William fretted about his sister's health, writing to a friend of how he first heard of her being sick: 'What a shock that was to our poor hearts! Were she to depart, the Phasis of my Moon would be robbed of light to a degree that I have not courage to think of.' He compared Dorothy's influence to that of his friend, the poet Coleridge: 'He and my beloved sister are the two beings to whom my intellect is most indebted.' In fact Dorothy outlived her brother. He died in

1850, while she continued in ill health; her dementia spared her from some of the grief of William's death. Their closeness continued: they are buried next to each other in the churchyard at Grasmere.

The story of Wolfgang Amadeus Mozart and his elder sister Nannerl is well known. At another time, with a different brother, Nannerl would have been acclaimed as a musical genius in her own right. But she was eclipsed as a child by her younger brother and while her relationship with her brother was full of bantering letters and affection, she was not treated as a musical equal. Fanny Mendelssohn, however, had musical abilities that were more comparable to those of her brother, but she was never under any illusion that her musical talents would be heard other than by friends and family. That honour was to go to her younger brother Felix, one of the most popular composers of the Romantic period. The two grew up in Germany playing the piano together (Fanny was born in 1804, Felix was four years younger) and they were judged to be equally brilliant. Fanny started composing as a young child but her father didn't think society was ready for women composers. In 1820, when Fanny was fifteen, her father wrote to her from Paris:

> *Music will perhaps become [Felix's] profession, while for you it can and must only be an ornament. We may therefore pardon him some ambition and desire to be acknowledged in a pursuit which appears very important to him because he feels a vocation for it, whilst it does you credit that you have always shown yourself good and sensible in these matters; and your very joy at the praise he earns proves that you might, in his place have merited equal approval.*

A less generous girl might have felt jealous of her brother's right to be the family's brilliant composer by virtue of being a man. Fanny didn't seem to feel jealous and she helped Felix because she loved music and adored him. Hours of making music together had made them exceptionally close. Their mother was heard to say, 'They are really vain and proud of one another.'

Felix relied on Fanny to criticise and refine his work. At the age of seventeen, Fanny wrote: 'I have always been his only musical adviser, and he never writes down a thought before submitting it to my judgement. For instance, I have known his operas by heart before a note was written!' On birthdays the

brother and sister gave each other gifts of musical compositions, which they often critiqued.

What saved Fanny from feeling that her talents were ignored
was her marriage to Wilhelm Hensel, an artist, who encouraged her to compose and perform her pieces. Felix was supportive of her in his own way. When Fanny fretted that she
couldn't compose after having a baby Felix reassured her that if
he had a baby under six months he would not be composing
either. 'Be thankful that you have him. Music only retreats
when there is no longer a place for her, and I am not surprised
that you are not an unnatural mother.' It was a kind and reassuring response to a new mother.

This sensitive nod to Fanny's maternal situation did not,
however, diminish Felix's high opinion of her as a musician.
Letters would tumble through the Hensel letterbox asking for
advice on what recital pieces he should play and how he
should develop his compositions. 'Can you point out to me the
various passages which struck you as particularly dramatic
when the idea first occurred to you? And above all say something more definite on the subject, as the whole tone and
colouring and characteristics take my fancy strongly . . .'

Felix's love for his sister was deep; his letters to her were
often effusive. In one birthday letter he wrote,

> *I thank God every day of my life for giving me such a sister
> as you . . . May you keep well and be as happy this and all the
> years of your life as you make all of us, especially me, who
> can never thank you enough for all you are and have been!*

However much Felix admired his sister's compositions, he
still didn't think it seemly for her to publish them under her own

name (he performed her music but did not attribute the works to Fanny). So when Fanny's mother and husband appealed to Felix to persuade her to publish her work he refused:

> *She is too much all that a woman ought to be for this. She regulates her house, and neither thinks of the public nor of the musical world nor even of music at all until her first duties are fulfilled. Publishing would only disturb her in these and I cannot say I approve of it.*

Fanny wrote over four hundred pieces of music in her lifetime, many of them songs. Eventually her resolve not to publish her work was broken by the money offered to her by music publishers. She wrote to tell Felix and waited anxiously for his reply. There was silence. It was the only time in their relationship that Felix upset his sister. When his letter did arrive it was conciliatory and generous in wishing her success. Fanny had less than a year to enjoy any public acclaim; she died of what sounds like a stroke at the age of forty-two while playing the piano. When the news was broken to Felix he fainted. Fanny's death was the only event in his life which interrupted his composing. He wrote to a friend, 'I have not as yet been able to think of music; and when I try to do so, all seems empty and desolate within me.' It may have been unrelated to Fanny's death but Felix died less than a year afterwards; the brother and sister are buried next to each other in a churchyard in Berlin.

The story of the Lambs is actually a heart-wrenching tale of a brother–sister relationship. Charles Lamb was a poet and essayist known for the children's book *Tales from Shakespeare* which he wrote with his sister Mary. The Lamb family had a history of mental illness and their home was modest and not terribly happy. Mrs Lamb was not an affectionate woman and had a favourite in her oldest son John, while she ignored Mary, who at ten years of age was left in charge of baby Charles. Mary was a loving sister, teaching her brother to read and missing him desperately when he went off to school. As they grew older their family life began to disintegrate: their father developed either dementia or a similar mental illness and their mother became an invalid. Charles was the first sibling to suffer depression, not long after falling in love. Details are hazy but the love affair never developed and in the winter of 1795 he became an inmate of what was known in less politically correct times as the 'Hoxton madhouse'. He wrote a poignant poem to his sister, apologising for any angry words he had said to her while his mind was unbalanced.

Tragically he was about to sign up to a lifetime of repaying his debt to his sister. Mary's mental health had been declining, linked to the relentless misery of doing needlework to help pay the family bills and watching over her infirm parents. On 22 September 1796 all the family apart from the two sons were in the sitting room, when Mary, then aged thirty-one, was suddenly enraged by something their young apprentice girl was doing. She grabbed a knife, chased the girl, and stabbed her own mother to death when she intervened. Charles, who arrived home at that moment, calmly took the knife from his sister. *The Times* recorded the coroner's court verdict that Mary was insane and she was put into a 'madhouse'. Charles assumed responsibility for his sister after his father died a few months later, and the two lived together in what he called 'double singleness' for the rest of their lives. For a young man of twenty-two this was a remarkable self-sacrifice. But when Mary was not mentally ill she was calm, sympathetic and a supportive sister whose company her brother enjoyed above anyone else's. On the first Christmas after the murder Mary again became aggressive and agitated and was admitted into an asylum. Charles wrote a plaintive poem to her, revealing his dependence on her, on Christmas Day. It starts:

> I am a widowed thing, now thou art gone!
> Now thou art gone, my own familiar friend,
> Companion, sister, helpmate, counsellor!

Throughout her life Mary had relapses, to the extent that her brother never took her out without something to use as a straitjacket. In 1805 he wrote to their friend Dorothy Wordsworth expressing his feelings when Mary was again admitted to an asylum. By this time he had, perhaps understandably, developed an alcohol problem.

Meantime she is dead to me – and I miss a prop. All my strength is gone; and I am like a fool, bereft of her co-operation. I dare not think: lest I should think wrong: so used am I to look up to her in the least and the biggest perplexity ... She is older, and wiser; and better than me, and all my wretched imperfections I cover to myself by resolutely thinking on her goodness. She would share life & and death, heaven and hell with me. She lives but for me. And I know I have been wasting and teasing her life for five years past incessantly with my cursed drinking and ways of going on.

When Charles was sober and Mary well, the two wrote together and had a rich literary social life, counting the Wordsworths and Coleridge as close friends. Their book *Tales from Shakespeare* was an instant success when published in 1807 and is still in print today.

As they grew older Mary's bouts of mental illness became more frequent and protracted and Charles wondered bleakly at times if she would ever recover, but she always did. She outlived her brother by thirteen years, although her mental health deteriorated substantially. They are buried together in Edmonton.

Charles Dickens's relationship with his sister Fanny was nowhere near as close but her death had a long-lasting effect on him. He could have been rather bitter about their relative childhood fortunes, as while his elder sister was allowed to study at the Royal Academy of Music he was sent to work in a bleak factory. But they were close as children and remained so when she married Henry Burnett and had a 'crippled' son, also called Henry. Both Henry and Fanny are drawn upon in *A Christmas Carol* to great effect, as Tiny Tim and his sister. But nothing is as affecting as Dickens's letter to his friend John Forster after seeing Fanny dying of consumption at the age of thirty-eight. For Fanny to have talked so frankly to her brother

about her innermost thoughts shows the depth of their closeness and their ability to confide in each other. Sadly, the real-
life Tiny Tim, poor Henry, died later.

A change took place in poor Fanny about the middle of
the day yesterday, which took me out there last night. Her
cough suddenly ceased almost, and, strange to say, she
immediately became aware of her hopeless state; to which
she resigned herself, after an hour's unrest and struggle,
with extraordinary sweetness and constancy. The irri-
tability passed, and all hope faded away; though only two
nights before, she had been planning for 'after
Christmas'.

She is greatly changed. I had a long interview with her
to-day, alone; and when she had expressed some wishes
about the funeral, and her being buried in unconsecrated
ground [her husband's family were dissenters], I asked her
whether she had any care or anxiety in the world. She said
No, none. It was hard to die at such a time of life, but she
had no alarm whatever in the prospect of the change; felt
sure we should meet again in a better world; and although
they had said she might rally for a time, did not really wish
it. She said she was quite calm and happy, relied upon the
mediation of Christ, and had no terror at all. She had
worked very hard, even when ill; but believed that was in
her nature, and neither regretted nor complained of it.
Burnett had been always very good to her; they had never
quarrelled; she was sorry to think of his going back to such
a lonely home; and was distressed about her children, but
not painfully so . . .

Such an affecting exhibition of strength and tenderness, in all that early decay, is quite indescribable. I need not tell you how it moved me. I cannot look round upon the dear children here, without some misgiving that this sad disease will not perish out of our blood with her; but I am sure I have no selfishness in the thought, and God knows how small the world looks to one who comes out of such a sick-room on a bright summer day. I don't know why I write this before going to bed. I only know that in the very pity and grief of my heart, I feel as if it were doing something.

Some famous brothers and sisters of our time have had trickier relationships. The film stars Shirley MacLaine and Warren Beatty are not often seen together, and many people do not realise they are brother and sister. This has led to speculation that there is animosity between them. It's impossible to know, as all there is to go on is what they say publicly, but it's not difficult to speculate why they might not be close. Shirley strongly believes in spirituality, and Warren is conventionally political and may think his sister's beliefs are frivolous. Shirley as the older sister by three years may also have resented the arrival of her handsome younger brother.

In an interview with Larry King in the 1990s, Warren was asked if there was a rift and replied, 'She's my sister. I love her.' He claimed he would have loved to work with her and that she felt the same way, but when King asked Shirley about wanting to work with her brother she replied, 'Well, I don't know if I could do sixty-three takes.' She had, she said, fought his battles for him as a child but also bossed him around. When asked by journalist Ginny Dougary about their relationship she said, 'I understand the workings of a family better now – brothers and sisters, sisters and sisters – I mean, come on. We're in a very good and cordial period now . . . I don't know how long it will last but we're there now.'

Shirley has not shied away from voicing opinions about her brother's life that may have been controversial. She was open about how she would have coped if Madonna, who dated her brother, had become her sister-in-law. 'I said it would be like hanging bubbles on a clothes line, or pissing up a rope,' she told Dougary.

Who knows what Madonna thought of Shirley, but she has had her own share of brotherly troubles. The singer, occasional actress and children's author was not pleased when her younger brother Christopher's *Life with My Sister Madonna* was published and much publicised. On one level it said nothing that even a fan of Madonna would not have acknowledged: that she is obsessed about her body, highly controlled and controlling, and addicted to fame. Christopher, who was three when his mother died, seems to have grown up intent on treating Madonna as a maternal substitute. As he describes it, Madonna was his father's favourite of eight children, the one who got his lap and the special dress for her confirmation. As she sought fame through dancing and then singing, she took Christopher with her, only to dismiss him as one of her backing dancers when her career took off. Over the years Christopher was picked up and let go at will, being his sister's dresser (wiping the sweat off her breasts during shows, reassuring her that her midriff was not fat and holding out his hand to catch her discarded cough sweets), interior designer for her houses and director of some of her world tours such as *The*

Girlie Show. He said he couldn't leave his sister, because he felt protective about her, however casual she was in her treatment of him. It was Madonna who publicly 'outed' him as gay, who paid him, as he repeatedly says in the book, peanuts compared with other designers, and who expected him to drop everything when she clicked her fingers. It was she who insisted he had a cocaine and alcohol habit and needed rehabilitation, while his own doctors thought at least part of his problem was his addiction to his famous sister. Madonna's celebrity status defined their relationship. Christopher referred to the enormous shadow of his sister's fame under which he lived, yet readily admitted to using Madonna's name to get into restaurants (in which he was then treated like royalty) and that he loved mixing with Hollywood actors. In the book he constantly mentions his sister's financial success and her relatively

parsimonious attitude to the rest of her family. By the end of the book the two siblings are distant. They've fallen out over his work on one of her houses: she thinks he is overcharging her, he thinks she is exploiting him. 'I've made you what you are,' she allegedly tells him in a mean-spirited email. With Christopher's main source of income gone, he can't afford the payments on his car and has two lodgers; she cites her income in 2002 as $56 million.

Christopher never pretends that his memoir is for the public good. Madonna snorts as she gargles each morning in the bathroom; she can spend two and a half hours a day in the gym but still, he says, has legs that look like 'fat sausages', and she demands white dressing rooms with white flowers. As a hatchet job it's not carnage, but more controlled revelation. Given the unbalanced nature of their relationship, it could have been worse, but you have to hope Christopher doesn't spend the advance for this book too quickly as Madonna may be even less likely to subsidise him in the future.

Jane and I shared everything. She was two years older than me. Still is, now I think about it. We never rowed, never bitched, did everything together, and always seemed to know what the other was thinking. I remember the first time it struck me. We were in Bournemouth on holiday, and looking forward to the evening bingo when she went down poorly – stomach ache, perhaps she'd eaten too many of the chocolate éclairs for afternoon tea. So she went to bed and Mum looked after her, and I went down with Dad for the bingo, and I just knew that evening she was going to win. Not just a line, but a full house. What's more – I knew the amount. Four pounds and ten shillings exactly. I was seven, she was nine, it was a year before decimal currency shook up the world.

And so it turned out to be. Four pounds ten shillings exactly. I'd promised her that's what she'd win, and when I went up to see her in bed and tell her, quite matter-of-factly, because I knew it was destined, that she'd won her four pounds ten shillings on the bingo, it cemented our bond.

A few years later, I got ill big-time. Two years in bed with leukaemia. When the doctors finally accepted I was ill and not just a malingerer, they made no secret of the fact they thought I'd die. Jane knew, but it was the first thing she didn't share. She didn't really invite friends home in these years. The house was dark, curtains drawn, mid-seventies, three-day week, you name it; our grandmas died; a time of permanent mourning. I didn't talk much in those times, but the little that I did was to Mum, Dad and Jane.

She became my pop proxy, though she wouldn't know it if you told her today. I was mad about pop music, read all the mags from the brainy *Melody Maker* to the cool *NME* to the more downmarket *Disc* and *Record Mirror*. I knew everything there was to know about music – except what it sounded like. The thing is, in those days my head hurt too much to actually listen to the stuff. So I'd read about it and decide what I liked from what the mags said about bands, and some I just liked from memory – Slade, T Rex, Bowie, the Sweet. Jane's job was to sing me the songs, so I could make an informed judgement.

'Jane, how does "My Coo Ca Choo" by Alvin Stardust go?'

And she'd try her best. She'd only do it for me because she wasn't a confident girl and didn't have much of a voice.

> 'Coo! Coo!
> I just want you,
> I really love the things that you do.'

'I like that,' I told her. 'I thought I'd like him because I've read up all about him. Great sideboards, and he used to be called Shane Fenton.' Then I'd ask Mum if she'd go and buy me the record from the shop on Cheetham Hill.

Jane knew I was mad about Bowie. One day she went

out and bought me a cassette of *Hunky Dory* without me even hinting to her that I'd like it. What a sacrifice – £2.75 it cost, five and a half weeks' pocket money. And what an album – it was 1973 now; the record was as old as Rome (it had come out in 1971), and full of these amazing songs I'd never heard – 'Changes', 'Oh You Pretty Things' (which I'd once heard Peter Noone sing on the Mike Yarwood Show), 'Life on Mars' of course, which had just weirdly been a massive hit (number three), 'Kooks'. Jane sang the songs to me, and I loved them. She had just started her period, so I changed the words of 'Ch-Ch-Ch-Changes' to 'P-P-P-Periods', which I thought was hilarious and poor reward for her generosity. The cassette sat on the shelf by my bed for months and months until I started listening to music again. When I finally played it, I was in Bowie heaven.

It was 1975 when I eventually went back to school proper, and we remained just as close. I had not seen my old friends for three years, and never saw them again until I grew up – and then only in passing. They didn't just belong to a different era, they belonged to a different life. When I went back to the comprehensive, I was in the second year of secondary, and I'd not been in a regular school since the third year of junior. Some of the kids had known me, or known of me, at the juniors. On my first day, as we were lined up outside the class, one boy, Jeremy, said to me, 'I thought you was dead.' Another said, 'Aren't you the lad who went mad?' Sometimes I laughed about it – sometimes I cried, usually with Jane. She wasn't finding teenage life that easy, either. Specs, ginger hair and dodgy boyfriends didn't help.

I made new friends quick enough, and brought them back home, and we shared them as we had done before I was ill. She brought her friends back home, and we shared them, too. Hers were two years older than mine, and they were girls, so I suppose that was a bit unusual but it didn't feel it. On Saturday nights when lots of kids were starting to go to youth groups or even clubbing, we'd go into town together. It was usually me and my best friend Rob, and Jane and any combination of three of her friends. We'd normally go to a burger bar called The Great American Disaster, and have burger and chips and hot chocolate fudge layer cake, then get the bus back home. We lived in Manchester, I was mad about music, things were beginning to happen with punk and Buzzcocks, but we were never trendy.

I was fifteen, and Jane had moved back into my bedroom. We'd chat til we went to sleep, gossip, eat shit, fart, tell each other blow-job jokes, listen to music – it seemed the most natural thing in the world. Dad didn't think so. He was embarrassed, thought it the most unnatural thing in the world. One day he said to us, didn't we think it was time Jane moved back into her bedroom and we laughed and called him a dirty old man, which he wasn't.

Rob had started to stay at our house more. He was tall then, and strong. He wore cotton bracelets and was funny. He was strong and girls liked him. He liked to fight, and every Saturday he insisted we had pretend fights in my bedroom that were quite painful, and even more frustrating because he always won. Rob lived in south Manchester, which felt like a thousand miles away even though it was less than ten and it was pointless going home. He loved our house anyway, so he'd stay for weekends. Sometimes in the week too. At times, I wasn't even aware he was around. I suppose he became like a brother. Which made what happened all the more painful.

I didn't notice them getting closer. Well, it was hard because they'd been close all along. And yes she'd ruffle his hair, and link his arm when we all walked out, but it was just a joke really, or chivalrous, or acting out what she'd be like with proper boyfriends. But then they started whispering and going off together, and being giggly and secretive, and I started to feel like a gooseberry because they weren't telling me anything. And this was Jane and Rob not telling me; the two people who had always told me everything.

I don't remember when I witnessed it the first time, all I know is I felt sick, and as if I couldn't breathe. Maybe because I wasn't breathing. By this stage the bed thing had got complicated. This is how I think it worked, though memory plays tricks. When Rob stayed here, Jane returned to her bedroom, and he stayed with me in the spare bed. When she thought I was asleep she would creep into my room, and get into bed with Rob. But I wasn't asleep. I was nowhere near asleep. All I knew is that I didn't want to be anywhere near my own bedroom, let alone hearing and half seeing what I was hearing and half seeing.

It was the slurps I hated most. The long, slurping kissing. I don't think there was that much more to it, though maybe I'm wrong. But it went on for ever, schhhlllurppp, schlurppppp, schlllurppppp. It reminded me of somebody eating loudly, and both Rob and Jane knew that noise went through me. I pretended to be asleep because it felt wrong to be awake, as if I was a voyeur in my own bedroom;

eavesdropping on my own betrayal. And that's what it was – a bloody betrayal by the both of them. And I'd try to think of City or Pink Floyd or the best volley I'd ever done, but I couldn't because all I could hear was the fucking schlurping, and occasionally I'd half open an eye, but no more because I was worried they'd think I was spying on them. And I couldn't see anyway because they were under the sheets, and Christ I didn't want to. After an eternity that might have been ten minutes, Jane would slip out and tiptoe back to her room. And I'd lie there wanting to scream and cry and puke.

It went on for months, and nobody ever spoke about it. It was their little secret. I think she thought it was wrong because he was her little brother's best friend, and she was terrified that Dad would walk in on them. Rob thought it was wrong because she was my big sister, and he was my best mate. I couldn't bring myself to mention it because somehow the whole edifice of everything would crumble. And it just hurt too much – physically. Whenever she got into his bed my adam's apple became inflamed and raw. Schhhllurlppp, schlurppppp, schlllllurppppp.

Nor can I remember when it stopped. She went out with the boy across the road, and I didn't care what they did together. Rob went out with girls, and I didn't care about them either. The equilibrium was kind of restored, but not fully. A trust had been breached. Even though he was still my best friend, it was different. For years I had nightmares – not about Jane, but about Rob. In all of them, he betrayed me or humiliated me.

One night Jane brought a friend home. Gillian was tall with short blonde hair and a broad Bury accent. She was

clever and smelt of perfume. We were all watching telly in
my bedroom, as was the norm when we had guests round.
Jane and Andrea were on the spare bed, and Gillian ended
up on my bed. She was backing into me gently as she
watched the telly, and I couldn't see the tiny screen properly but I didn't care because I could smell her hair and
perfume. I'm not sure how we ended up holding hands, let
alone how we ended up kissing, but I am sure that we were
pretty discreet about it. We certainly didn't flaunt it, and I
don't think we even schlurped in an excluding way. We
waited for Jane to go to the loo to kiss, and her mouth
tasted of honey and mustard, and her neck was warm as
Majorca.

Gillian slept in Jane's room, and I certainly didn't creep
into her room in the middle of the night. Next day we
didn't pretend nothing had happened. We held hands, and
it felt like we were an old couple. Gillian left in the morning, and after she had gone I played 'Ever Fallen in Love
with Someone (You Shouldn't've Fallen in Love With)' by
Buzzcocks repeatedly and very loud on my music centre,
and told myself that love was the absolute bollocks. Jane
was cold and remote, but she didn't say anything. She
never invited Gillian home again.

Two years later, I started university in Leeds. On my first
day I went into the wrong lecture theatre and sat down,
realised I was in the wrong place, and looked at the student
next to me. It was Gillian. I'd not seen her since she had
stayed with us. We didn't know what to say, so we grinned
like idiots. 'I think we should split up,' I said. She laughed.
But I don't know why I said that because that was the last
thing I was thinking.

It took me the best part of twenty years to tell Jane and Rob how much their thing had screwed me up. For the first time since we were kids, we all got together last year. All of us, with our respective partners and children. Jane worried that I had felt left out, but it was fine. Rob and I are friends again – when I introduce him to other friends, I tell them 'This is Rob. He was my best friend til he slept with my sister.' He says it pisses him off, and that I should stop doing it. I don't know what happened to Gillian. I still love *Hunky Dory* and 'Ever Fallen in Love'.

10

Fairy-tale Sisters

Fairy stories have been passed on through generations, enchanting, terrifying and entertaining old and young. In these stories are a wide range of human characters: there are the wicked, the good, people who are generous, envious, those who are wronged and those who get their just deserts. And among them are sisters. Fairy stories were never just make-believe but reflected real life, even if they seemed incredible. So the everyday business of sisterhood is displayed in extreme ways in fairy tales. Sisterly jealousy can lead to murder; sisterly devotion to self-sacrifice. Fairy stories have been told all over the world, many of them with common themes and characters. The best known in Europe were collected by the Brothers Grimm in *Household Tales*.

The most famous 'sister' story is that of Cinderella, who in the Grimms' version (and there are many variations world-wide, of which the first is a Greek story in the first century BC) has two beautiful stepsisters – not ugly at all – who are 'vile and black of heart' and make her work for them all day long. Her father goes on a trip and asks the three sisters what presents they would like. The stepsisters want dresses and jewels, but unworldly Cinderella requests the first branch that knocks against his hat on the way home. In this story the branch is watered by her tears from her maltreatment by her sisters, and grows into a tree in which lives a little white bird which grants her wishes. Cinderella goes to the prince's ball and wins his heart. When he comes to find the owner of the slipper she has left behind on the stairs in her rush to get home, her stepsisters cut off bits of their feet to try to fit into it. But bloody feet were not nearly enough gore for a Grimm fairy tale, and so when the stepsisters pitch up for Cinderella's wedding, pigeons peck out both their eyes. This fairy tale has attracted much academic and feminist discussion; its themes of sibling rivalry and cruelty, the unnatural attachment of a stepmother, displacement of the motherless child and the prince as saviour on a white horse have all been pored over. There is the obvious comparison of the good sister and the wicked sisters. This theme is present in many fairy tales, although sometimes the bad sisters are merely lazy and thoughtless rather than incredibly cruel. The psycho-analyst Bruno Bettelheim in his essay on sibling rivalry in 'Cinderella' said that the story was a way for children to recog-nise and resolve their envious feelings. He argued that fairy tales are a good way for children to come to terms with life's adversities and their own anger and anxiety. Characters are polarised in fairy tales: there is a good or bad sister, not one who is a bit of both. This makes it easier for those hearing or reading the stories to get the moral.

Often there are three sisters in fairy stories; the two eldest are usually the baddies and the youngest is the undemanding, selfless one. In 'The Three Sisters', the youngest sister Nella is beautiful and talented and thus envied by her jealous sisters. Her sisters, says the story, 'desired to put her underground'. A prince who falls in love and secretly visits Nella is fooled by the sisters into hurting himself so badly that his life is in the bal-ance. This being a fairy tale, the antidote is the fat of an ogre, which the brave Nella procures for him by slicing up some local ogres and getting him to drink their fat. The prince proposes to her and throws her sisters into an oven, thus proving, says the fairy tale, 'No evil ever went without punishment.'

In an Italian tale three sisters, again through the brilliance of the youngest, get the better of the devil who has married them each in turn and pushed the elder sisters into a fiery abyss. The youngest pulls them out and they escape by tricking the devil into carrying them to their parent's house. When he realises the youngest sister is missing he runs to the house only to be faced with the three sisters standing on the balcony laughing at him. This terrifies him so much 'that he took his flight with all possible speed'.

One fairy tale particularly stands out in its portrayal of sisterhood. The story of Snow White and Rose Red is one of sisterly love, which their mother encourages. The sisters are different; Snow White is quiet and devoted to their mother, while Rose Red likes running around outside. The story paints a perfect picture of sisterhood:

> The two children were so fond of one another that they always held each other by the hand when they went out together, and when Snow White said: 'We will not leave each other,' Rose Red answered: 'Never so long as we live,' and their mother would add: 'What one has she must share with the other.'

One day there is a knock on their cottage door and when Rose Red opens the door a bear walks in. Their mother tells them to stop screaming and soon the bear is made so comfortable that he becomes a regular visitor. When the spring comes he says

goodbye, as he has to leave to guard his treasure from a wicked dwarf. The story ends with the sisters walking through the heath and rescuing a dwarf from the clutches of an eagle. Unknown to them the dwarf is the very villain who has now stolen their beloved bear's treasure. When the bear appears the ungrateful dwarf urges him to kill the sisters, but the bear despatches the dwarf instead. Handily the bear has been under a spell and turns into a handsome prince. He marries Snow White, while his brother marries Rose Red. Their old mother comes and lives with them. The moral of this story is clear. Good things come to sisters who love and watch out for each other.

11

Celebrity Sisters

It can't be easy to have a celebrity as a sister. As an ordinary mortal you may have a job you enjoy, a partner you love and a modest suburban house, and given human nature you may not be deliriously happy but at least moderately satisfied. Yet how would you feel if each time you opened a newspaper or switched on the television your sister was there, swanning down a red carpet to the latest film premiere, or locked in an embrace with a famous hunk on a Caribbean beach? You've got similar genes, probably had the same upbringing, so why is it her, and not you?

What distinguishes a celebrity from a non-celebrity sister may be her determination, a small difference in bone structure, talent or luck. A sister who has a celebrity sibling will find it hard not to live in her shadow, inevitably being compared and sought out for gossip. But sometimes the celebrity sister has forged ahead because of their own sibling rivalry, to prove that she should be the one their parents favour. Anyone with a celebrity sister has the chance to trade off her, either by selling a story about her or being given the hand-me-downs of fame. There seems to be a feast of celebrity sisters in the early twenty-first century. Some, like the actresses Nicole Kidman and Penélope Cruz, have sisters who are also stunning and success-ful, but just not as famous as they are. The actress Sienna Miller has teamed up with her sister Savannah to produce a clothing label. There are sisters within the same family who both want to be celebrities, although it's not always clear what they are famous for (apart from having famous parents). The Geldof sisters Peaches and Pixie may adorn catwalks and have aspirations to be taken seriously but like the Hilton sisters (of hotel fame) it is their outrageous behaviour that attracts media attention. Other sisters such as Jackie Collins and her sister Joan have overlapped in their careers, although Jackie is best known for her blockbuster novels (she tried acting at one time) and Joan for her film and television roles. They have consistently denied any rivalry.

When there is rivalry between a celebrity and her sister it can be vicious. An early example is that of Maria Callas, who was the first operatic diva to be acclaimed throughout the world. Her sister Jackie called her biography *Sisters*, leaving no doubt that this was a book about her as much as her sibling. Jackie was six when Maria was born in 1923 and she was thrilled to have a sister because her mother (who was Greek) was strict and a snob. Now Jackie had an ally to cuddle and play with. So far so good. Their mother wanted

Jackie to be a pianist but it was Maria who took over the instrument to accompany her own singing. Their mother began to see Maria as the family meal ticket, and pushed her into a singing career, but still favoured Jackie. Maria was to say in an interview with *Time* magazine in 1959:

> My sister was slim and beautiful and friendly, and my mother always preferred her. I was the ugly duckling, fat and clumsy and unpopular. It is a cruel thing to make a child feel ugly and unwanted ... During all the years I should have been playing and growing up I was singing or making money. Everything I did for them was mostly good and everything they did to me was mostly bad.

This doesn't chime exactly with Jackie's memory but both sisters felt their mother exploited them. When their mother took the girls back to her home in Greece, she encouraged Jackie to become the mistress of a wealthy man who could subsidise Maria's early career.

After Maria's singing career soared their relationship changed into a mixture of loving protectiveness and petty competitiveness. The contrast between the dumpy teenager with the glorious voice and the sister whom men gravitated towards was still marked until Maria moved back to America and became a diva. Jackie had hoped for some recognition as Maria's sister, but Maria was determined to shrug off her family. Neither Jackie nor her mother shared in her success. Jackie watched from a distance while Maria lost weight, became a much-photographed beautiful star and had an affair with Greek shipping magnate Aristotle Onassis. After Maria died from a heart attack, quite suddenly in 1977 at the age of fifty-three, Jackie recalls sitting by her dead body in her apartment in Paris. Her thoughts show how her sister's success diminished her own life:

> . . . it still seemed impossible that that slim figure, that beautiful angular face could really be Mary Callas, dumpy Mary Callas, spotty Mary Callas stuffing her face with food before hurrying off to high school in Washington Heights. Now her face was beautiful, her hands so long and fine . . . She had had everything in the end. I had been the beautiful one, I was the sister who would marry. Mary, dumpy, fat-legged Mary would sing. Now there I was sixty and unmarried and there was Mary, one of the most famous women in the world, married, divorced, the victim of one of the most famous affairs of all time. It was unfair.

But wait a minute, you might ask, poor Maria's dead now, isn't she? Jackie says that she has asked God to forgive what Maria had done to her but anyone reading the biography is likely to think the apology should come from Jackie.

Any sister might have felt eclipsed by Marilyn Monroe but her half-sister Berniece Baker managed to avoid feeling jealous.

This may have been because Berniece was nineteen when she was told she had a half-sister and Marilyn (then Norma Jeane) was twelve. Their mother was mentally ill and at various times abandoned both girls. During Marilyn's lifetime Berniece never talked to the press and kept a low profile, but after her sister's death she wrote a memoir called *My Sister Marilyn* which is so measured that you believe her when she says she did it to 'speak the truth about Marilyn'. Pictures of the sisters show a family resemblance. Berniece describes their first meeting, at a train station, before Marilyn was famous:

> . . . She stood out immediately from all the rest of the passengers, so tall and pretty and fresh. We were excited to finally meet, and we couldn't stop staring at each other. We had the same dark blond hair with a widow's peak, the same mouth, but our eyes were different – mine are brown and Norma Jeane's were blue like our mother's. I was so happy to have a sister. And so proud.

The Marilyn in her memoir is thoughtful, determined and a perfectionist.

> At the end of our telephone calls, I always told Marilyn I was proud of her and that I loved her. And so often she would repeat to me as we said good-bye, 'Please promise me you won't give out stories about me.' And I would always say, 'I promise.' I had vowed to myself that I would never be a troublesome relative. I wanted to do exactly as she asked.

When needed, Berniece would drop everything to look after Marilyn, but she was on holiday when her sister died and only heard of it two days later. She has always said her sister would never have killed herself, and that her overdose must have been an accident. In her will Marilyn left money (the first that had ever exchanged hands between the sisters) for Berniece and for the cost of their mother's nursing care.

The actress Nicole Kidman's relationship with her sibling seems unaffected by her celebrity status. This may be because the Kidmans are a grounded and politically aware family, who have managed to raise sisters who seem supportive and fond of each other, to the extent that Nicole's film-star status is irrelevant to their relationship. As children they were so close they had a secret language, and the media is full of reports of them rushing to each other's side when anything significant happens. When Nicole divorced Tom Cruise; when she married Keith Urban (her sister was her maid of honour); when Urban went into rehabilitation for drug and alcohol problems; and when she had her baby, Antonia was always there. Likewise when Antonia split with her husband, had her first birthday after her separation, and needed support with her children, Nicole flew thousands of miles to be with her. Antonia has a respectable career as a journalist and television presenter but it is nothing like as successful as her sister's. Even so, there seems to be no rivalry. In a newspaper interview Nicole said that Antonia was her best friend. 'We've been through a lot together, she and I. For a long time, we were each other's sole source of comfort.'

Rumours of sibling rivalry between celebrity sisters are often exaggerated, perhaps because stories of mutual support sell fewer newspapers. Joan and Jackie Collins are both famous in their own right, and perhaps because Joan has played sexu-

ally avaricious women and Jackie has written about them, they have not been thought of as particularly close. Yet although the age gap between them made them distant as children, once Joan went off to Hollywood and Jackie started writing bodice-ripping blockbusters (starting with *The World Is Full of Married Men* which in 1968 was rather shocking), their careers and lives became more entwined. Joan credits her sister with helping her when her film career stalled in the 1970s. Jackie's book *The Stud* had a part which was made for Joan; all she needed was for her sister to write the screenplay for her. Jackie, who had never written a screenplay before, churned it out for her in six weeks. Her sister's career took off again. Annie Leibovitz took an iconic picture of the two sisters in the back of a limousine, both looking impossibly and equally glamorous.

In an interview Jackie expressed surprised that anyone had ever suggested there was rivalry between them. 'We're the best of friends,' she said. Joan in turn has said, 'I don't trade off her name, she doesn't trade off mine. You will never find us bringing up the other one unless someone brings it up for us.'

If the secret to sisterly happiness in the world of celebrity is to keep yourselves relatively separate, the Redgraves might be expected to struggle to avoid sibling rivalry. Actors Vanessa and Lynn both came from a family where acting was in the blood; their father Michael Redgrave was a Shakespearean actor. Both sisters were nominated for Best Actress Oscars in 1966, losing out to Elizabeth Taylor, and the following year shared the cover of *Time* magazine. During their long and illustrious careers Vanessa and Lynn fell out over some of Vanessa's outspoken political views. While co-starring in Chekhov's *Three Sisters* Lynn was reported as saying that her sister's political grandstanding over the Gulf War was 'driving me crazy'. This, along with a remark that Vanessa saw herself as a 'martyr', might have rocked their relationship, but as they grew older and Vanessa flew to New York to support her sister when Lynn had breast cancer, they recovered their previous closeness, walking in Central Park together and remembering their childhood. Lynn, the younger by six years, recalls her sister's generosity to her as a child; how she would illustrate tiny books for her dolls and how one Christmas when Lynn was six Vanessa gave her one of her own presents, a glass Bambi that she coveted for her own glass animal collection. Lynn promptly dropped and smashed it. In a recent joint interview she remembered how kind her sister was and how she comforted her. As they have grown older, they said, they both cherish their relationship and tell each other everything. They had, they remarked, returned to the intimate relationship of their childhood. When Vanessa's daughter Natasha Richardson died following a skiing accident in March 2009 it was Lynn's turn to support her sister.

The pop star Britney Spears may have had her own difficulties (requiring drug rehabilitation and losing custody of her two children after bizarre behaviour) but she fell out with her younger sister after Jamie Lynn became pregnant as a teenager. It seems that celebrity sisters expect their siblings to behave better than they do. She is reported to have told friends: 'I warned this girl. I really did. She seemed to take my advice. I'm really disappointed in her. I told her over and over just to be a kid and let the adult things like sex and drinking wait.'

In fact the story of Britney and Jamie Lynn is one of sisters who were pushed into show business as a means of pulling the family out of poverty and have since struggled to lead normal lives. It was harder for their ambitious mother to encourage Jamie to sing and dance because she was a tomboy. She was also, she has said, her mother and father's 'little baby' who was the most spoilt of the Spears children. Ironically Jamie Lynn was in a Nickelodeon show playing a virginal teenage girl when she became pregnant. Britney did go to see the baby, although reportedly only for one day.

For sisters who have no reason to share the media spotlight other than the fact that their sibling is a celebrity, the media can be thoroughly unforgiving. Victoria Beckham, formerly one of the Spice Girls (in its time a girl band that was a global brand) and wife of David, a footballer, model and icon of manhood, has made front-page news just by changing her hairstyle. So pity her poor younger sister Louise, less polished but with a pronounced resemblance to her superstar sister. The media have delighted in unflattering comparisons of the two.

In the biography of Victoria by Sean Smith the sisters' memories of school are intriguingly different. Victoria has spoken out about being bullied at school as part of her story of triumphing over adversity. This bullying has been attributed to her father dropping her off in a Rolls-Royce, her seeming snootiness and her claims that she would be one day be famous, which everyone found irritating. She also had acne. Whereas she remembers teachers walking her to the school gates for protection, Louise has said, 'I don't think she was bullied that badly. She got a bit of verbal abuse, but it wasn't anything major.' It seems that Louise and her sister were rather different; whereas Louise had lots of friends, Victoria was shy but full of self-belief. They rowed at home but remained fond and supportive of each other even as Victoria's career took off. When Louise's marriage broke up, Victoria was by her side, and Louise supported her in turn when David was accused of having first one and then other affairs. The sisters are often pictured out together. Newspaper reports claim that Louise has had plastic surgery at the same clinic as her sister and at times has copied her sister's hair colour. It's unclear why this should be remarkable. 'She loves the limelight as much as Victoria,' a 'friend' has been quoted as saying. As is the case with many sisters of celebrities, she is unlikely to get as much of it shining on her.

When one sister achieves cult status, as has been the case with Cheryl Cole, a singer in the band Girls Aloud, a judge on the popular *X Factor* talent show and virtually a national treasure, it is only a matter of time before the media starts seeking out the rest of her family. If they were hoping for a skeleton in her closet they found more than one. Cheryl is the epitome of a perfectly styled, beautiful young woman. Her appeal, however, comes from her straightforwardness and self-deprecating nature. The public love her because she seems authentic, still speaking with the Newcastle accent that she grew up with. There was a clue to her background when she was convicted of drunkenly assaulting a toilet attendant in a club. Born Cheryl Tweedy, she was brought up in Newcastle on a tough estate, on fish fingers, beans and chips and neighbours' hand-me-downs. Fighting to get your way was part of life. She has two elder brothers, an elder sister and a younger brother; two of the siblings, Gillian and Andrew, were born only a year apart and were inseparable. Cheryl says part of her desire to sing and dance was for them to notice her. Their mother was not initially truthful about Cheryl's relationship with her elder siblings. Cheryl was eleven when she found out they were really half-siblings from her mother's first marriage. The lives of her siblings reflect what could have happened to Cheryl; her brother is addicted to glue and has over fifty convictions, for mugging, theft and a stabbing. He and Gillian had a public fight that resulted in a court appearance in 2002 (after going out drinking to celebrate Cheryl's success in *Popstars: the Rivals*, which launched her career). A friend on the estate died of a heroin overdose. Both Gillian and Andrew remain consistently loyal to Cheryl; not for them a spiteful sibling exposé for a few thousand pounds in a tabloid newspaper. Andrew has been quoted as saying that Cheryl has done everything she can to help him, including visiting him in prison. 'Cheryl wants to help me, but I'm too far gone . . . I watch Cheryl on TV and think, "Your life is so different to the one you left behind."'

Gillian has said she does not talk to the media, which has not stopped the press comparing her unkempt mousy hair, single-mother status and run-down house to Cheryl's glamorous looks and mansion. An article in a celebrity magazine said there had been jealousy between the sisters but that Cheryl had offered to help her sister financially, an offer which had been refused. Despite the public fracas with her brother,

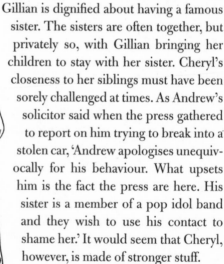

Gillian is dignified about having a famous sister. The sisters are often together, but privately so, with Gillian bringing her children to stay with her sister. Cheryl's closeness to her siblings must have been sorely challenged at times. As Andrew's solicitor said when the press gathered to report on him trying to break into a stolen car, 'Andrew apologises unequivocally for his behaviour. What upsets him is the fact the press are here. His sister is a member of a pop idol band and they wish to use his contact to shame her.' It would seem that Cheryl, however, is made of stronger stuff.

The background of the Winslet family was somewhat different from Cheryl's. Kate Winslet, one of Britain's most successful actors, had parents who had set up the Reading Repertory Theatre Company

and an uncle who had acted in the West End. She and her sisters, Anna, three years older, and Beth, three years younger, took part in productions at school and the local youth theatre, went to London to see shows and dreamed of life on the stage. Whether by luck or talent it was Kate who got the breaks, despite being called 'Blubber' at theatre school for being overweight. It's hard to imagine how her sisters feel about her stardom; why it's her and not them collecting the prizes. Yet there is not a whisper of sibling rivalry, even though the press like to draw attention to Kate's sisters' less prestigious acting jobs. When Anna did a theatre tour on a barge named the *Titanic* – the title of the film that made Kate's career – newspapers swiftly picked up on it. The day that Kate won her first Oscar, a British newspaper ran a picture of Beth fiddling with the tyres on what was said to be her run-down car. The paper delighted in comparing Beth's baggy jeans and modest acting career with her sister's glamorous A-list status and numerous awards. When asked about sibling rivalry in an interview, it made Kate rather cross. She has certainly denied it emphatically. 'I will swear on my entire family's life that I have never, ever, ever, had a problematic relationship with any of my family members. We're incredibly close.' But she has admitted to feeling guilty about her success. 'I think, Christ, why can't I share this out?' It seems only a matter of time before, like the Redgraves, the Winslets will be wanting to perform *Three Sisters* together.

If you love chess you will have heard of the Polgár sisters. Susan Polgár and her two younger sisters, Zsófia and Judit, were raised by their parents to be chess champions. Their father, László, believed that geniuses were made, not born, and he set out to prove it, using chess as the example. The girls were taught at home in Hungary, and their father must have packed a lot of chess tuition into Susan's early years, because she won her first chess tournament at the age of four. In 1984, when she was fifteen, she was the top-ranked woman in the world. She was the first woman to be named Grandmaster of the Year, in 2003, and during her career won many Olympic medals and championships. She now directs the Susan Polgár Institute for Chess Excellence and teaches youngsters, especially girls, how to play the game. Her two sisters were also prodigies. Zsófia, five years younger than Susan, won a major tournament in Rome at the age of fourteen, defeating several Grandmasters, but was less committed to a chess career. Judit, the youngest by two years, is regarded as the best female chess player in history. At the age of ten she defeated an International Grandmaster and went on to win major titles like her sisters. The sisters played chess at a time when women had not been allowed to play against men and had to fight hard to be accepted on to the 'male' chess circuit.

Susan Polgár on her sisters

We were all home-schooled so we were different from typical families. It made us closer because we spent twenty-four hours a day with each other. When we played chess we had a common interest and when we started travelling to tournaments we always had each other. It was an excellent time. We had a wonderful relationship because we were close friends, not just sisters. We are still very close but we live in three different countries now so we are less close than we used to be.

I remember my sisters when they were little. Particularly Judit, she was seven years younger than me and I remember her coming home from hospital with very red hair. I used to change her diapers. I didn't resent her when she was growing up because she was so sweet and good-hearted. By the time Judit started playing chess I was already a master. I encouraged both of my sisters to play; I taught them for thousands of hours during the years when we didn't have tutors. We have talked about our upbringing but we have taken the attitude that we can't change it anyway. When we talk about it we think we had adventures and excitement growing up. We can say with a hundred per cent certainty that we had more eventful lives than most young girls. We travelled a lot, we went to Europe, Asia, Australia, all over the world; it wasn't a boring life.

But we had a modest childhood. Things were more restrictive in communist Hungary. It gave us less temptations and options, so chess was one of the few things we would do in Hungary to excel in and get a better life. We played five to six hours of chess a day but we also played table tennis and had other lessons. In the beginning when my parents tried to get us a permit for home schooling it was highly unusual and they had a big fight with the authorities. Our parents kept appealing against the rulings and eventually the authorities gave in and we got the permit. The police came round and tried to get us to go to school but my parents always resisted.

I think we are very different but we had a strong common bond that few sisters have. It is unusual to have a common lifestyle and profession. Our family was our world. We had common friends through chess. Sisters will usually have different friends and different interests from each other. Chess connected us. We had common challenges when we represented Hungary in the Olympics – when your sisters represent your country with you that's unique. People talk about the Williams sisters but there are only two of them.

I had my first big success at four and a half when I won the Budapest girls championship. I was exposed to the media early on and so I knew I was different but my upbringing was always normal to me because I didn't know any differently. It was even more natural for my sisters because they had my example.

It was lovely to teach Judit. When she won the Hungarian National Chess Championship she was only fifteen and it was one of the proudest moments of my life. It was a family triumph, an incredible victory. She proved that men are not superior to women. It was a big achievement far beyond chess even, and it was so extraordinary because she was a woman and she was only fifteen. She was the first woman to win a national championship.

It helped me to have sisters on a social level because they were company for me. Chess wise they also helped me after a while, but because of our birth order, Judit and Zsófia benefited more and they really only helped me towards the end of my competitive career.

We did face discrimination which is why it was better that we were the Polgár sisters rather than individual women playing chess. In Hungary thirty years ago it was not so simple to enter tournaments as a woman, they were for men. Women weren't welcomed and it was a challenge to be able to play. In 1986 I qualified to play in the men's world championship but I wasn't allowed to play because they said it was called the men's championship.

It's hard to tell if we could have been good at anything. I suppose our father thought we could have been. We are different in looks and personalities; even though we have the same attention and education we have different personalities. Zsófia is not as diligent a chess player as Judit and I am, she enjoyed lots of other things. She is the middle child; she retired from competitive chess to raise her two children. We don't speak as often as I'd like but we do see each other. It is always lovely to see each other. We shared so many experiences of growing up together. She is five and a half years younger than me. Judit is very firm, she knows what she wants. From a young age she was more decisive.

My sisters are probably still the closest people to me; if I had a problem I would go to them first. I liked having my two sisters. But my sisters may not have felt the same. Zsófia was the middle child and I was always better than her because I was older and then Judit passed by her, so she was sandwiched between us. Perhaps she felt left out. In any other family Zsófia would have been a star in her own right. There was some rivalry, we trained together a lot but we always felt we were fighting for a bigger accomplishment, such as trying to be able to compete with men, than we were fighting to win for ourselves. We had so many other rivals as well that it didn't matter so much about each other. We knew it was up to us to change the world of chess. For Judit it was something monumental for a woman to do as well as she did, it went beyond family rivalry.

There are other chess prodigies but no other group of

three sisters who have been as successful as we have been. Over twenty years either Judit or I led the world rankings. For many years Zsófia was in the top ten too.

We understand that there are very few people out there you can count on. If you have a sister you are very fortunate because if you have a trust between you it is irreplaceable. Rarely do we play chess together. We have too many other priorities, such as our children, to talk about when we meet each other.

12

Royal Sisters

Few fathers could have done such a ham-fisted job of promoting sisterly love as King Henry VIII. Admittedly when Elizabeth Tudor was born on 7 September 1533 at Greenwich Palace her father had recently divorced his first wife, Catherine of Aragon, and left the Catholic Church, so there was nationwide upheaval. But the effect her birth had on her elder half-sister Mary was devastating. Henry wrote to Mary immediately after the birth, telling her that she was now no longer Princess of Wales (because her baby sister was) and that she had to agree that his marriage to her mother had been unlawful. As a finale she was to accept that his marriage to Anne Boleyn (which much of England opposed) was lawful. Mary was seventeen years old. The loathing she had for Anne Boleyn and the blame she laid on her for destroying her mother's life was lifelong and readily extended to Elizabeth. When, in December, having refused Henry's pleas to accept his new marriage, Mary was moved into the household of her baby sister and told to pay her respects, she burst into tears. She knew, she said, of only one Princess of Wales, and that was herself.

For one mother and child to flourish the standing of the original two had to be reduced. While Anne and Elizabeth were feted in court, Catherine was given draughty lodgings in less salubrious quarters to live in. It must have given Mary considerable pleasure when Anne plummeted from grace. Anne's execution for adultery in 1536 effectively put Elizabeth in the same situation as Mary, although her position was even more vulnerable because Europe recognised Mary as the only legitimate heir to the throne.

Henry, keen to treat both sisters equally badly now, made both Mary and Elizabeth illegitimate under the 1536 Second Act of Succession but still treated them as princesses, although they were known as the lady Elizabeth and the lady Mary, followed by a quick 'the king's daughter'. Even after he married Jane Seymour and finally had his male heir Edward, Henry stubbornly refused to resolve the issue, but his will laid down that if Edward died Mary would be next to the throne and if she died without heirs then Elizabeth would become queen. As adults it was Elizabeth who grew up to resemble her father more obviously than Mary did.

By the time Henry was on his sixth wife, Katherine Parr, Mary and Elizabeth had little contact. Elizabeth was close to her younger half-brother Edward and together they were brought up to be Protestants. Katherine Parr gave Elizabeth a huge advantage over her sister by educating her to a standard that was exceptional for women. Elizabeth was intelligent but her education, by some of the most distinguished tutors in England, gave her the edge over Mary. What also gave Elizabeth an advantage in her relationship with Mary was her attitude to religion. Catholicism defined Mary with a deep fervour, whereas for Elizabeth, Protestantism was just a religion.

Henry died when Elizabeth was thirteen and Edward ten. Edward's court was supportive of Elizabeth; she was seen as his 'sweet sister temperance', a contrast to his Catholic sister

Mary, who dressed flamboyantly and refused to accept Edward's religious policy. Elizabeth, mindful of Edward's serious ill health and her sister's position in the succession, wisely let her sister and brother fight it out between them.

In the background was John Dudley, the Lord Protector, who as Edward lay dying convinced him to give the throne to Lady Jane Grey. Had the succession passed smoothly to Mary, her relationship with Elizabeth might have remained both distant and dangerous for her younger sister, whom Mary had never trusted or liked. Dudley managed to get Lady Jane briefly on the throne but failed, despite threats, to make Elizabeth renounce her claim. She cunningly insisted, 'You must first make this agreement with my elder sister during whose lifetime I have no claim or title to resign.'

As soon as Elizabeth heard that Lady Jane Grey had been arrested and that her sister was queen she left her sickbed and came to London. She had not seen Mary for five years. When they met at Wanstead the sisters hugged and kissed each other, but after the initial warm greeting it was too difficult for Mary really to embrace Elizabeth. Political manoeuvring meant there were many at court to remind Mary of Elizabeth's role in her misery and to suggest she may be plotting to undermine her. Elizabeth wisely moved to Hatfield House with the strategy that being out of sight would mean she was out of Mary's mind. Every time there was some criticism of Mary's reign, it was inevitable that Elizabeth would be the focus for any opposition. Yet Elizabeth was anxious to behave in a sisterly fashion to Mary, writing to her (and in turn receiving letters from her sister) and enquiring after her health.

An impartial observer at the time, the Venetian ambassador,

described their relationship and the differences between the sisters rather accurately. Of Mary he said:

> In her youth she was rendered unhappy by the event of her mother's divorce; by the ignominy and threats to which she was exposed after the change in religion in England . . . She is, moreover, a prey to the hatred she bears my lady Elizabeth, and which has its source in the recollection of the wrongs she experienced on account of her mother, and in the fact all eyes and hearts are turned towards my lady Elizabeth as successor to the Throne.

Of Elizabeth he wrote:

> Her father's affection she shared at least in equal measure with her sister, and the king considered them equally in his will, settling on both of them 10,000 scudi per annum. Moreover the queen, though she hates her most sincerely, yet treats her in public with every outward sign of affection and regard, and never converses with her but on pleasing and agreeable subjects.

Their relationship suffered in the aftermath of Mary's marriage to the Catholic king Philip II of Spain. When a rebellion led by Thomas Wyatt was foiled by Mary, a letter was intercepted supposedly from Wyatt to Elizabeth. Mary's government summoned Elizabeth to London for questioning. Elizabeth denied anything to do with the rebellion, and in genuine shock and distress at the accusation asked to see her sister. Stephen Gardiner, the bishop of Winchester, who was interrogating her, told her she was destined for the Tower of London. Elizabeth was terrified and begged to write a letter to her sister, which Mary in fact refused to read. The letter, of 16 March 1554, shows how terrified Elizabeth was; how she believed her sister might really order her execution:

If any ever did try this old saying, 'that a king's word was more than another man's oath', I most humbly beseech your Majesty to verify it to me, and to remember your last promise and my last demand, that I be not condemned without answer and due proof, which it seems that I now am; for without cause proved, I am by your council from you commanded to go to the Tower, a place more wanted for a false traitor than a true subject, which though I know I desire it not, yet in the face of all this realm it appears proved. I pray to God I may die the shamefullest death that any ever died, if I may mean any such thing; and to this present hour I protest before God (Who shall judge my truth, whatsoever malice shall devise), that I never practised, counselled, nor consented to anything that might be prejudicial to your person anyway, or dangerous to the state by any means. And therefore I humbly beseech your Majesty to let me answer afore yourself, and not suffer me to trust to your Councillors, yea, and that afore I go to the Tower, if it be possible; if not, before I be further condemned. Howbeit, I trust assuredly your Highness will give me leave to do it afore I go, that thus shamefully I may not be cried out on, as I now shall be; yea, and that without cause. Let conscience move your Highness to pardon this my boldness, which innocency procures me to do, together with hope of your natural kindness, which I trust will not see me cast away without desert, which what it is I would desire no more of God but that you truly knew, but which thing I think and believe you shall never by report know, unless by yourself you hear. I have heard of many in my time cast away for want of coming to the presence of their Prince; and in late days I heard my lord of Somerset say that if his brother had been suffered to speak with him he had never suffered; but persuasions were made to him so great that he was brought in belief that he could not live safely if the Admiral lived, and that made him give consent to his death. Though these persons are not to be compared to your Majesty, yet I pray to God the like evil persuasions persuade not one sister against the other, and all for that they have heard false report, and the truth not known. Therefore, once again, kneeling with humbleness of heart, because I am not suffered to bow the knees of my body, I humbly crave to speak with your Highness, which I would not be so bold as to desire if I knew not myself most clear, as I know myself most true. And as for the traitor Wyatt, he might peradventure write me a letter, but on my faith I never received any from him. And as for the copy of the letter sent to the French King, I pray God confound me eternally if ever I sent him word, message, token, or letter, by any means, and to this truth I will stand in till my death.

Your Highness's most faithful subject, that hath been from the beginning, and will be to my end,

ELIZABETH.

I humbly crave but only one word of answer from yourself.

It took so long for Elizabeth to write the letter that the tide had turned and the trip up the Thames to the Tower had to wait until the next day. Elizabeth spent two long, frightened months in the Tower and although her sister was put under immense pressure to execute her by some of her advisers who were desperate to safeguard Britain from a Protestant monarch, Mary refused to do so.

It was Mary's husband Philip who did most to save Elizabeth. He knew that executing her would be enormously unpopular, even cataclysmic for Mary. So Elizabeth's release from the Tower was Philip's work, as was her reconciliation with her sister. As Mary lay, supposedly in late pregnancy (the baby never materialised and is likely to have been an ovarian growth), Elizabeth was graciously allowed to see her. Before doing so she was urged again by Mary's ministers to confess that she had been disloyal and offended Mary. Elizabeth, while careful not to criticise her sister, denied it outright. When she did meet Mary she had the sense to fall on the floor dramatically

and swear that she was innocent. It was the gesture that her sister was looking for. The supplication restored Mary's sense of superiority and she was so pleased with her sister that she allowed her to live relatively freely at Hampton Court. As Mary later lay dying the temptation to appoint another successor must have been great. Mary had always felt Elizabeth lay in wait and distrusted her because of that.

It was largely thanks to Philip's influence and to her own popularity with her people that Elizabeth assumed the throne to outshine her sister as a queen of England. After her death James I built an elaborate tomb for her in Westminster Abbey, where somewhat ironically her resting place is next to that of her sister. Had Elizabeth and Mary known that James's epithet for them would be: 'Partners both in throne and grave, here rest we two sisters, Elizabeth and Mary, in the hope of one resurrection', they might not have rested so peacefully.

Before Elizabeth there were two sisters (one of which was her mother) close to her heart who had their own sibling rivalry. Anne and Mary Boleyn shared the bed of King Henry VIII at different times, but little else. Mary, the eldest sister, was born around 1508 and Anne a year or so afterwards. Their brother George, who got on with Anne much better than his less intelligent sister Mary, was born in 1503. Mary's legacy is of being 'the other Boleyn girl', the one who was Henry's mistress but not smart enough to become his wife. History records Mary's relationship with Henry as the more fortunate one. Mary was the more docile, more beautiful yet less animated sister, though with a reputation for fecklessness and easy virtue (so not exactly dull).

The girls were daughters of Sir Thomas Boleyn, Henry's

ambassador in the Low Countries. Both spent time in France at the court of the king's sister, Mary Tudor, who had been married off to the old and sickly Louis XII. Mary is rumoured to have had an affair with Louis's son Francis and perhaps with others (she was known as the English Mare in the French court), and returned home to be rehabilitated by her ambitious family. As part of this rehabilitation she was swiftly married to Sir William Carey in 1520, although sources vary as to whether she married him before or after her relationship with Henry. It was around 1519 or 1520 that Mary caught the eye of the English king, who arranged for her to join the court of his wife, Catherine of Aragon.

Henry was fairly generous to Mary during their affair, which started when Mary was around seventeen years old. Anne, who was accustomed by her forceful personality to being the most notable member of her family, was jealous of her sister's position. She was also dismissive of Mary's management of the affair, believing her to be too guileless to exploit her position. The affair did not continue for long – two years – and some time afterwards Mary had a child whom she called Henry (but who was almost certainly her husband's and no relation to the king). When Mary's husband died of 'sweating sickness', Henry appointed Anne, who by now had him in thrall, as the guardian of her nephew. In a love letter to Anne around this time he referred to Mary's loose morals as a potential source of embarrassment to them and bad influence on her own son. There is no record of Anne's reply.

The queen, aware of Anne's refusal to become the king's mistress, noted the fundamental difference between the sisters. Anne was the Boleyn sister the queen most feared, for as she pointedly said to her, 'My lady Anne, you have good hap to stop at a king but you are not like others, you will have all or none.' The reference to others who had succumbed to the king's charms without holding out for the main prize included her sister Mary.

When Henry contrived to marry Anne after going to such extreme lengths as divorcing his wife and extracting England from the Catholic Church, Anne made her sister a lady-in-waiting. What Mary really wanted was a happy domestic life. Secretly she married a man called William Stafford without asking permission, which, as the sister of the queen, she was obliged to do. Anne was furious (and undoubtedly embarrassed) and certainly did nothing to stop Mary and her husband being banished from court. William was not a man of means and the couple rapidly fell on hard times. Mary contrasted her own choice with her sister's husband. William, she said, was honest and truly loved her: 'I had rather beg my bread with him than to be the greatest queen in Christendom.' Anne did help financially but the sisters don't seem to have seen each other again. When Anne plummeted from grace Mary did not visit either her sister or brother (who was also accused and executed, although innocent, for incest). Mary's absence only reflected common practice. When your relatives were facing execution it was best to keep out of the way. History does not record Mary's feelings about her sister's death but she must have been shocked by the loss of both her siblings. Sadly she didn't live to see her sister's daughter Elizabeth become queen of England. This niece was kinder to Mary's relatives than Anne had ever been.

Between the Tudors and the monarchy in Britain today there were other royal sisters who bickered and played

together, loved each other at one moment and felt the pain of competition the next. In royal life roles are determined by accident of birth. Elizabeth and Margaret Windsor were two such sisters. One was destined to grow up in the limelight, the other, who had the more extrovert personality, forced to stand just off centre stage. The princesses were, from necessity, each other's best friends. They rarely saw any other children and would play together for hours with outsized gifts such as the lavish playhouse given to them by the people of Wales. Elizabeth was born in 1926, the first child of the Duke and Duchess of York, and had four years before her already disciplined life was interrupted by a baby sister. As a young child Elizabeth's life was rigid and dictated by royal protocol: waving from carriages and learning to control any normal but undisciplined childish behaviour. The birth of her sister Margaret relieved the pressure in some ways but also highlighted the differences in what was expected of them. Elizabeth had to be serious and focused on royal obligations, whereas Margaret was more indulged and allowed to have a laugh. They were in many ways treated fairly and almost too identically, being dressed in the same clothes and learning the same things, whatever their aptitude might have been for other activities.

Their governess Marion Crawford ('Crawfie'), who was later vilified by the royal family for writing her memoirs, claims that Margaret wanted whatever her elder sister had. To get it she was capable of throwing a punch at her sister and, when that failed, biting her. Both girls were competitive but while Margaret shone at music and anything artistic, Elizabeth prevailed at being the more regal. With King Edward VIII's abdication, the parity of their upbringing was abruptly ended. Elizabeth was, after all, the next in succession after their father. When she told Margaret that this meant she would be the next queen, Margaret apparently said, 'Poor you.'

Elizabeth, at eleven, was now living at Buckingham Palace and privy to her father's despatch boxes and discussions about politics. She became increasingly restrained and responsible. Worse, as far as Margaret was concerned, was that she started telling her off. Margaret was not to laugh at anyone in public, or to be casual when meeting and greeting in crowds. Elizabeth once chastised her for rustling her prayer books too loudly. Crawfie claims that Margaret resented Elizabeth's position and felt distinctly second best, the spare to the heir, despite being the more outgoing and attractive of the two. To Margaret it seemed she had all the obligations of royalty but would have none of the glory. Yet Elizabeth had her own feelings about the fairness of their relationship. While she was being groomed relentlessly for the job of queen, she could see her younger sister had the freedom to express herself and to be petted in a way that she never was. But the biggest challenge to the sisters' relationship was typically nothing to do with the succession, but was over a man.

When Elizabeth married Prince Philip in 1947, her sister was genuinely happy for her, even if she felt displaced as her sister's companion. When, after the death of their father (which Margaret was deeply upset by as she was his favourite), Elizabeth became queen, Margaret resigned herself to supporting her sister from the sidelines. But when Margaret fell in love and wanted to marry the divorced Peter Townsend, whom she'd met when he had been the king's equerry, it was her sister who effectively stood in the way of a happy-ever-after ending. The queen would not have been able to give her formal permission because Townsend had been divorced, but she made it clear that she would not oppose Margaret's right to be happy. Papers released from the National Archive show that the deal that was offered should Margaret have chosen to marry Townsend was more generous than reported at the time. Margaret would have had to give up her right to the succession and get married in a registry office but would not, as rumoured, have had to live abroad. Even so there was to be no marriage. Margaret, who loved Townsend and had known him for many years, felt she could not marry him with such restrictions. Elizabeth, while she was only obeying governmental procedures, still felt culpable, although Margaret never believed it was her sister's fault. Margaret went on to marry Antony

Armstrong-Jones, whom she later divorced, and for many years she dominated the gossip columns. Unlike her sister, she had no real role in life. Elizabeth must sometimes have shuddered at her sister's unsuitable liaisons and louche behaviour. Yet Margaret always saw herself as primarily a monarch's sister. When asked by the media about her role, she said, 'In my own sort of humble way I have always tried to take some part of the burden off my sister. She can't do it all, you know. I leap at the opportunity of doing lots of different things to help.' Her divorce, however, did not help her sister; it was notable in being the first royal divorce since Henry VIII's. She and Elizabeth, however, still remained close, with Elizabeth always feeling the elder sister's protective instincts towards Margaret When Margaret died, Elizabeth spoke of her 'beloved' sister who had served her country. It may have been a eulogy by a monarch, but it had the heartfelt sentiment of a sister.

While Elizabeth and Margaret largely embodied the traditional ways of royal sisters, recent siblings have chosen more wayward paths. In Monaco Princesses Caroline and Stephanie have played out their lives in the media in a way that might have shocked even Princess Margaret. Caroline was born first, followed by Albert, and it was Stephanie as the baby of the family who was most spoilt by their parents, Princess Grace and Prince Rainier, and who turned out to be the most outrageous sibling. Grace had been a Hollywood movie star and Stephanie was thought early on to have her mother's outgoing personality. Caroline, as the elder sister, was expected to be the responsible one. This inevitably meant that Stephanie and Albert became close in the face of their sister's bossiness. Stephanie said that Caroline always treated her like a kid sister but

Caroline had her own gripes; Stephanie was the only child
allowed to watch television on school nights and was excused
from tidying her bedroom. Caroline, however, was the first to
upset her parents seriously, by marrying Philippe Junot, who
had a reputation as a playboy. Stephanie may have been
impressed by her sister's marriage but the union only lasted
two years.

When Princess Grace was killed in a car crash, the family
was overwhelmed by grief. Stephanie, who was in the car with
her mother at the time, was badly injured and unable to attend
the funeral. In the years that followed both sisters sought
refuge in relationships; Caroline married again and, when her
husband was killed in a speedboat accident, became increasingly involved in the commitments of the royal family, working
with charities and attending functions as the first lady with her
father. She went on to marry Ernst V, Prince of Hanover, a
respectable choice and watched with considerable disapproval
as Stephanie took a series of somewhat less conventional partners. Stephanie had an affair with Anthony Delon, the son of
an actor, who had a history of car theft and gun possession;
she also had a liaison with Mario Oliver Jutard, who had
been accused of rape, and she got engaged to a man who was

SOME PAST LOVERS

a convicted fraudster. Her choice of husband trumped her sister's poor choice; she married her bodyguard after having two children out of wedlock, only to divorce him a year later. Then there was an elephant tamer, her father's butler, a Portuguese-Spanish trapeze artist and a married croupier. Caroline most certainly did not appreciate her sister's bizarre choice of men, or excuse it, as some did, on the grounds that she had never got over Princess Grace's death. The rest of the family may have been more relaxed about Stephanie's love life but Caroline, in a reprise of her role as elder sister, put her foot down. While Stephanie was seeing her father's butler, Caroline forbade her to attend any official functions, the climax of this ban occurring on the eve of a Red Cross gala ball. Stephanie had already bought her dress for the occasion but Caroline called together her father and brother and insisted that her sister had tarnished the family name enough. *Paris Match*, claiming reliable sources, said that Caroline had issued an ultimatum to her father saying she would not share a ballroom with her sister. On the night of the ball, Stephanie was otherwise engaged. *Vanity Fair* published an article saying that Stephanie had told a friend the ban was due to Caroline's jealousy of her.

With their father now dead and the sisters older, their relationship may have mellowed. Their poor brother Albert, now king of the tiny principality, must hope he is not called upon to settle any sisterly spats.

13

Criminal Sisters

There have been some shocking sisters. In this chapter are sisters who did terrible things together, encouraging each other to commit crimes that include the grisliest of murders. The private worlds that these sisters inhabited were terrible, lonely places, built together because they either had no family support or were confronted by a hostile world. In the aftermath of their crimes psychiatrists have tried to unravel how these sisters constructed such alternate, desperate lives for themselves, writers have put forward their own interpretations and arguments have raged over whether they were victims of their social circumstances or just bad.

The story of the Papin sisters has reverberated throughout France since the evening of 2 February 1933 when they brutally murdered the wife and daughter in whose house they were employed as maids. The latest film about them, *Murderous Maids*, was made in 2000; their crime holds a timeless fascination.

Emilia, Christine and Léa Papin were the daughters of a mill worker, Gustave, and a shop assistant, Clémence. They had a miserable upbringing; their parents were estranged, Christine was brought up by an aunt and Léa was taken in by an uncle when their parents finally divorced. Emilia and Christine were then sent to an orphanage and 'house of correction' in Le Mans. Emilia made an excellent decision to enter a convent as soon as possible and was therefore not involved in the horror that took place later. Christine found a job as a live-in maid and once Léa was old enough they looked for work together. The Lancelins took them both in and they worked for the family for six years. Mme Lancelin and her daughter Geneviève barely spoke to them, but this was probably not unusual in dealings with domestic servants. The sisters became intensely close, obsessively so since they only had each other for company. Their social isolation was partly through choice but also because live-in maids generally did not get out much. They also had no family ties, having chosen to cut themselves off from their mother, who had barely been involved in their upbringing. Reports of the case at the time said the sisters were not only extraordinarily absorbed in each other, but also sexually involved (although the sisters denied this). Christine was the more intelligent and dominant sister.

There was never any suggestion that the sisters were systematically ill-treated by the Lancelin family but there was one alleged incident where Mme Lancelin pinched Léa to get her to pick up some paper she had dropped. On the night of the murder Mme Lancelin and her daughter had gone out for the evening and M. Lancelin was also not at home. The only trigger that could be identified for the attack that night was the fuse going on an iron that Christine had already had to pay to be mended. When the Lancelins returned to find the house in darkness the Papin sisters launched a savage attack. If you are squeamish read no further. The sisters battered them to death with hammers, removed some of their clothing, slashed their thighs and ripped out their eyeballs, leaving them macabrely on the stairs. They then retired to bed, where they lay cuddled together, telling the police when they arrived, somewhat unconvincingly, that Mme Lancelin had attacked them and they had acted in self-defence.

The sisters were kept in jail separately and initially refused to eat or drink. Christine was overtly disturbed while awaiting trial and tried to tear out her own eyeballs. In court, hard though it is to believe, three psychiatrists for the prosecution said the sisters were responsible for their actions and deserved no mercy. A psychiatrist for the defence, however, pointed out the bizarre chasm between the brutality and violence of the murder and the absolute lack of motive and suggested more psychiatric testing was needed. His advice was ignored and as the court case continued it became obvious that Christine was the instigator and Léa had been caught up in her madness. Léa was sentenced to ten years' hard labour and Christine to the guillotine, although this was changed to hard labour for life despite Christine refusing to appeal. Léa did appeal but was refused. Christine's mental illness became too florid to be ignored and she was transferred to an asylum where she died three years later from a chest infection. When Christine saw her sister before being moved to the asylum she did not know her, saying, 'She is very nice but she's not my sister.'

Léa on her release went to live with her mother and spent the rest of her life as a domestic servant, doing the same work that she had done with her sister, living in draughty bedrooms, lonely and quiet. During the court case some communist commentators argued that it was the bourgeois French family that should be on trial. The sisters were portrayed as innocents caught in the class struggle. Simone de Beauvoir was, like much of France, deeply affected by the sisters' case. She argued that this was a class crime, that maids like the Papins were being humiliated by their employers every day and that the responsibility for the crime lay with the sisters' terrible childhoods and the bourgeois families of France. However, even she was driven to admit that Christine was paranoid and Léa was deluded.

The crimes committed by the Gibbons twins were relatively minor in comparison but the tragedy of their lives was just as great. In her compelling book *The Silent Twins*, Marjorie Wallace paints a haunting picture of sisterhood going horribly wrong. June and Jennifer Gibbons were born uneventfully in 1963. Their parents had emigrated from Barbados (their father Aubrey joined the RAF) and settled in Wales with the twins and their two elder children. Their mother Gloria was overtaxed by having four small children and by the RAF habit of moving personnel around, making it difficult to put down roots. From an early age the twins wanted to do everything together, and although they did not speak more than a few indistinct words, by the time they went to school Gloria was not worried. She had another child, Rosie, and even by the time the 'twinnies', as she called them, were getting school reports at the age of eight that said they wouldn't talk or do any work, she still believed they were just late developers. When the family moved to Devon the twins were badly bullied by other children because of their dark skin and strange speech. They withdrew even more into their isolated world with their bizarre, rapid speech, playing for hours with dolls in their room and refusing to speak to anyone in their family except their youngest sister Rosie. Their games with their toys were not the usual ones; their dolls were assassins, they robbed shops and murdered their parents. The twins adopted strange behavioural patterns, and their teachers saw a destructive bond between them, whereupon a glance from one could moderate the other's response. They walked in a disturbing, exaggerated way one behind the other. When the twins were eventually sent to see some experts at the request of the school medical officer, the speech therapist noticed how June wanted to talk but that Jennifer stopped her by the slightest of eye movements. 'The thought entered my mind that June was possessed by her twin,' she reported.

Attempts by various therapists to unlock the twins' exclusive and increasingly unhappy world failed and as a result, at fifteen, they were separated for the first time and sent to different boarding schools. They refused to eat and after five weeks they both absconded. Their teachers and parents gave in and allowed them to stay together, although there were signs that the twins themselves were feeling desperately trapped and frustrated. June more than Jennifer gave indications of wanting a more normal and independent life.

At home they tyrannised the rest of their family, ruining their

elder sister's wedding by being mute, and they refused to enter
the sitting room for years. They left school with no prospect of
getting jobs and spent their days at home, compulsively writing
stories and plays, all based in America with anti-heroes and
highly dramatic plots littered with sex and violence. Their
typewriter inflicted its own tyranny on the family as the twins
pounded relentlessly on the keys into the early hours of the
morning. They took their writing seriously, sending out
manuscripts to publishers, which were all refused. This constant rejection wore them down and at eighteen they changed
direction for a while, pursuing boys (sons of soldiers from the
US Army base near by) and becoming obsessed with losing
their virginity. In keeping with their ritualistic behaviour the
twins both attempted to have sex for the first time with the
same young man, who only managed to complete the act with
Jennifer. This made June intensely jealous but it seems to have
also further destabilised her sister. One night shortly afterwards Jennifer tried to strangle her sister with a cord from their
radio. June wrote:

> Something like magic is happening. I am seeing Jennifer for
> the first time like she is seeing me. I think she is slow, cold,
> has no respect and talks too much; but she thinks I am the
> same. We are both holding each other back. She does not
> want jealousy or envy or fear from me. She wants us to be
> equal. There is a murderous gleam in her eye. Dear Lord, I
> am scared of her. She is not normal. She is having a ner-
> vous breakdown. Someone is driving her insane. It is me.

The 'insanity' affected them both. The girls, strangers to convention, dressed oddly and looked unkempt, didn't make eye

contact or speak, and their favourite pursuits were, in no particular order, boys, alcohol, glue-sniffing and bingeing on sweets. They followed boys relentlessly, knocking on their doors, posting messages and allowing them to grab at their bodies in alleyways and deserted playgrounds. Their unstructured lives became more sordid, while their parents seemed oblivious to the effect they were having on the local community. Now that the twins were obsessed with being noticed they committed pitiful petty crimes that usually involved throwing a brick through the window of a school or shop and taking things they didn't want. The next step was arson. Since the police seemed unable or unwilling to arrest them, they attempted a burglary right in front of a local constable. Finally they were locked up, and while they waited for their case to come to court they alternated between violently attacking each other (it was not uncommon for them to draw blood), being separated and then being reconciled. They wrote copiously, thousands of words a day in tiny writing in flimsy prison

notebooks. It is the twins' writings that help to make them so fascinating; externally they seemed to want to be identical, to merge into one person. But in their diaries their accounts of what happened to them each day are not identical, neither are their feelings about each other. Much of what they write is so vivid and insightful that it seems incredible that no one could help them.

Incredible, too, that they were diagnosed as psychopathic and sent to Broadmoor, with promises that they would be helped. They were treated with tranquillisers, anti-psychotic drugs (used to treat schizophrenia) and behavioural modification, which included being threatened with being sent to another, more severe special hospital. The twins were punished by being kept apart (when they would often try to harm themselves), although when they were together they would often lash out at each other. Their resistance to conforming, especially to speaking, made staff resentful and uninterested. The mute twins were exasperating and the ultimate in defiance. It took nearly ten years for them to be released to a small unit in Wales. Marjorie Wallace, in writing the account of the twins' lives, had become one of the few people they trusted and spoke to. When she saw them just before their move she noticed Jennifer was thin and looked flushed. The sisters had agreed that should one of them die the other would start talking and try to lead a normal life. They had even told Marjorie that they couldn't become independent unless one of them died, and that they had decided Jennifer would 'sacrifice' herself. Within hours of leaving Broadmoor, Jennifer did die, suddenly, from a viral infection causing an inflammation of her heart. Jennifer seems to have been frail before her release. June was deeply upset but was quite clear that she felt she had been released from the prison of being a twin. She returned to living near her family.

Wallace's book had made the sisters famous and in 2000 a *New Yorker* article quoted June on her feelings about her sister's death. 'I used to miss her. Now I've accepted her. She's in me. She makes me stronger. I accept that she's gone now.' Her poem 'We Two Made One', in the collection *September Poems*, shows the conflicted love/hate relationship they had with each other.

WE TWO MADE ONE

A life
Our life
Always together, forever
Drawing strength from one another
Two beds, two heads, one mind
locked in
locked up
creating stories
inventing life
you and me
you are me
I want to find a part of me
That doesn't belong to you
a poisoned mind
this is our game
virgins on the dole

trying a little witchcraft
trying to be invisible
someone is driving you insane
it's me
stares and signals
my perception, your perception, clashing
you are me
you and me
a passing breeze across the sky
dreaming
separated
burning inside
this is our war
this is our life
who will give in
you or me
a division within and between
separated
only one should lose
I was missing from the world
You gave my life back to me
this is our life
this is our game
we once were two
we two made one
we no more two
through life be one

Another set of twins who felt they couldn't live with each other were Jeen and Sunny Han from California. So strong was this feeling on Jeen's part that she tried to kill her twin and in 1998, at the age of twenty-five, was sent to prison for twenty-five years. The story was quickly taken up by the media as it had the sensational components of beautiful twins, intense sibling rivalry and attempted murder. The Hans were born in South Korea and were brought to California by their mother when they were twelve years old. Their mother was often out gambling and the twins, like the other sisters in this chapter, relied heavily on each other. When they reached the age of sixteen their mother gave up any pretence of looking after the girls and sent them to live with an uncle and aunt. The girls did well at school but as they grew older their lives began to be as out of control as their mother's had been. Jeen graduated from high school and briefly pursued a career in the air force before deciding it was too regimented and exacting. She then worked in a casino, ran up her own gambling debts and stole credit cards and forged cheques (from family and friends) to try to repay the money. After being arrested for forgery she violated her probation by moving away to live with Sunny. It may have been that Jeen felt she had no other choice (they were no longer close as she had barely spoken to Sunny after joining the air force) or that she chose to run to the only person she felt she could rely on. Sunny, like her sister, had also been stealing. They seemed unable to escape the neglect of their upbringing and once together fought each other so often and so viciously that the police got used to being called to separate them. Jeen may have resented Sunny's more stable lifestyle (she was working as a receptionist) but the violence was mutual. On one visit to the house the police realised they had a warrant for Sunny's arrest – she had stolen and used a friend's credit card – and she was promptly arrested.

From here on the twins either acted in a most unsisterly fashion or else showed the darkest side of sibling rivalry. Jeen took advantage of her sister's incarceration to steal her credit cards and car, and when Sunny was released she promptly pressed charges. Jeen took off but rather than apologising, or attempting to repay the debt to her sister, she began approaching strangers and asking if they would help her to hurt Sunny.

Eventually she found two teenagers who were willing to try to murder her twin and took them to Sunny's apartment, along with some incriminating domestic cleaning products (presumably to remove bloodstains), duct tape and gloves. One teenager tied up Sunny and her flat-mate up at gunpoint while Jeen made off with Sunny's driving licence and withdrew money as fast as she could. The police caught both teenagers (Sunny had man-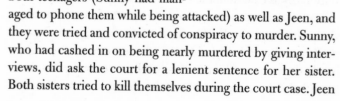aged to phone them while being attacked) as well as Jeen, and they were tried and convicted of conspiracy to murder. Sunny, who had cashed in on being nearly murdered by giving interviews, did ask the court for a lenient sentence for her sister. Both sisters tried to kill themselves during the court case. Jeen did not get a lenient sentence and on appeal her sentence was not reduced. The ruling said, 'Her actions were plainly adequate to demonstrate an evil design against her twin'.

Sisters can indeed be strange creatures. On 4 August 1892 a murder in Fall River, Massachusetts, became infamous throughout America and beyond. The case was that of Lizzie Borden, who was the main suspect in the murder of her father and stepmother. The murder weapon was a rather unfeminine hatchet and the murder so violent that her father's skull was split open.

Prior to the murder the family had not been getting on well. The Borden sisters, Lizzie and Emma, lived in separate parts of the house from their father and stepmother. The sisters were angry about their father's intentions to divide up his property among relatives before his death. One house had already gone to relatives of their stepmother's. Lizzie and Emma had argued bitterly with their father and both left the house for an extended break. Lizzie returned early. On the morning of the murder only Lizzie, her father and stepmother and the maid were at home. Lizzie called to the maid to say her father had been murdered, and while Lizzie was being comforted by neighbours the maid found Mrs Borden's body. Lizzie was tried for the murders and acquitted, despite having told contradictory stories. She was widely believed to be guilty and was cold-shouldered by their neighbours. Whether Emma believed her sister's innocence or had condoned the crime, she was sisterly enough to move into a new house with Lizzie. Remarkably, while the murders did not cause any sisterly disruptions, the two finally fell out over a party that Lizzie held for some actor friends. Emma was said to be unhappy about Lizzie's relationship with the actor Nance O'Neil, which was rumoured to be sexual at a time when being lesbian was thought of as badly as patricide. Emma moved out of the house. The two were not reconciled. Strangely, when Lizzie died of pneumonia in 1927 her sister Emma died from a fall less than two weeks later.

14

A Wider Family of Sisters

In today's society many sisters will not belong to the same family unit for their whole lives; they will be reconstituted into 'blended families' with stepsisters and half-sisters. This may happen when they are young or as adults. The acquisition of new sisters may be inconsequential or deeply affecting. And what of girls and women who have no sisters? Elizabeth Fishel in her book *Sisters* argues that there is a primitive and profound need to be and have a sister:

> It is a wish for someone to be as involved in our own process of figuring out who we are as we are involved in theirs: that person who is that mysterious combination of exactly like and exactly unlike ourselves, that mystery which we spend a lifetime trying to decipher and define.

Women who have strong relationships with their sisters may want to recreate this feeling with friendships outside the family; for others, that need has already been fully met. Those who have a poor relationship with their sisters, who find it hard to like them, may strive to create a sisterly relationship with a friend.

There is a wide experience of having stepsisters (not forgetting poor Cinderella) but one of the most powerful and beautifully written accounts is Jane Alison's memoir *The Sisters Antipodes*. When Jane was four her parents met another couple who were a mirror image of themselves. Within months the couples had embarked on affairs, exchanged partners and began divorce proceedings. Both families were torn apart and as Jane puts it, 'rearranged'. She and her stepsister began a grim, fierce battle for their own identities and the love of their absent fathers. In this interview Jane explains the lifelong fall-out from this terrible split:

We lived in Australia. Our parents were Australian diplomats and the other couple were American diplomats. In this exchange both couples had two daughters the same ages. The American diplomats were on a posting in Canberra and about to return to Washington and the Australians were coming back from Washington, so people said why don't you meet? The men were handsome and smart, the women were beautiful, there was an all-around attraction. My mother used to say it was so extraordinary to meet another couple and to be so attracted to them. Nine months after they met my parents divorced. It was a public divorce and I believe it caused some scandal at the time.

My counterpart was called Jenny and my name was Jane and she had the same birth date as me only she was one year older. My first memory of Jenny was at this girls' grammar school. I have this vague memory of having a scuffle at the top of the hill and either I pushed her or she pushed me. I had an older sister and Jenny had an older sister and later each couple had little boys within a short time of each other. It was extraordinary how the families continued to mirror each other.

Because of Jenny I felt I was replaceable, we had the

same everything: fathers, grandparents, half-brothers, names and birthdays. It was a bizarre version of stepsisterhood. It isolated the pure form of the feeling you often have as a replaceable daughter in any stepsister situation.

It is a great mystery how the swap between the couples happened. My mother had always said to me that 'it all seemed it was going to be all right.' It gradually became clear to me as I became an adult that it hadn't been all right and that my father and his wife were still angry and that my mother felt hurt whenever she heard my father was angry. It was confusing to work out who had wanted what. They all had different stories which I am sure were true but they were different.

After they did the rearranging my father went off with his new family and my sister and mother and I joined my new stepfather in America. For seven years we didn't see my father because we were living in different countries. My first clear memory of Jane was when we met again when I was eleven and she was twelve. My mother and her husband's marriage had broken up and we had returned to Washington. When we came back to America I think my sister and I were in shock that there was going to be another divorce, we felt we'd been left twice, mum was trying to work and we were about to start at a tough public school and we were blitzed, disorientated.

For the first time we were all on the same continent as my father had a posting in New York. My sister and I went to New York to see him.

I didn't go to see my father with any clear consciousness about having a stepsister, although of course I knew this: I

was just disoriented and vague that summer. It was like
having my eyes peeled open. I was put in a bedroom with
Jenny and everything changed. Jenny and I had way too
much in common. She had my last name now, and I had
hers: she had the same gifts my father had sent me over the
years. She and I both called my father 'Daddy'. She had
pictures of her father who had just been my stepfather. We
played and fought all the time, we were way too competitive. We'd compete over word games and who could do the
best cartwheels, we'd stay up all night doing cartwheels
and limbers and flips. We arm-wrestled. Then the stakes
went up and up. We never articulated the problem but she
had my father and I had hers.

I remember that when I met Jenny again on one of the
first nights together, sleeping in her room, she said: 'Who
do you think did it first?' The affairs couldn't have been
simultaneous and fair. I believe that between the two of us
we were trying to know which mother was the more sexually powerful and which father would leave his daughter,
because this was an indication of what each of us was worth.

One of the first things Jenny said to me was, 'It's terribly important to Daddy to treat all of us the same.' Whereas her father did not treat everyone the same: he liked a good race and especially liked the winner. I don't know why my father was bent on treating us all the same. Over the years when we didn't see him, my father had sent pictures of himself with his new girls. So I think we fought either for our own or each other's father.

So much of my book is about the horror of being so replaceable. There is the fear of not existing if you are replaceable. I am still destroyed by jealousy, which I am sure is related to these early experiences; it runs through my veins and if you light a match I will still flame with jealousy.

It had been hard to win my stepfather's love. I tried everything I could to be loved by him. I feel that at a certain point I looked at him and he looked at me and I decided I would do whatever it took to be his girl if he would be my dad. For the longest time I felt my stepfather looked through me and saw Jenny. I did drastic things to make him love me, to take a place in his heart. My mother would say, 'He's very fond of you because you remind him of Jenny.'

Jenny was smart and talented and for the longest time we competed to be the smartest and best and then I started to do better. I was winning prizes; I was Valedictorian at junior high school. Maybe it was her personality but by the age of thirteen she became destructive.

I feel guilty because when she got into trouble I became her father's confidante. I'd greet him when he came round to pick up his little boy and I'd give him a beer and he'd say what do you think about Jenny, what do you think she really wants, and I would sit with him and we'd talk it over and I would say, 'Well obviously she wants attention.'

She came to live with her father when she'd given up on high school and he rang me and said, 'I want you to be her model. I want you to show her how to have it both ways: how to get the grades and have fun.' I felt pleasure and thrill and terror. So I had her over and took her out with my friends and on our birthday, when she turned eighteen and I turned seventeen, we had a party. She slept with my boyfriend; well if you were her you would do, wouldn't you.

It's funny, she would come over and we'd go to parties and we drank a lot and smoked and she would sit in a dark corner and write poems and she'd ask me to read them and I didn't want to read her stupid poems. They probably weren't stupid; I know one of them wasn't because I saw it.

When she came over she slept in my room. She was interested in oceanography and I was interested in ento-mology and so we talked about crustaceans for hours at night. She was interested in fairy tales, I was interested in mythology. We were stuck together. Jenny used to call us Snow White and Rose Red – fairy-tale sisters bound together. It was mixed, dark, love and hate. Her mother would say that she just loved me but you don't sleep with the boyfriend of someone you love. Her dad didn't help because whether or not he said the actual words, the mes-sage he gave her was, 'Why can't you be more like Jane?'

It looked as though Jenny and I were on different sides of the same mirror, we were so alike, and then her side darkened. I don't know why, she was smart and talented. She was drinking and fucking around, well there were a lot of people doing that, but it was when she dropped out of high school that she came to live with my stepfather. After a while she went back to studying, it seemed like a push–pull thing. Jenny was trying to make as much of herself as she could then give up and destroy herself again. She started cutting herself and when she slept with my boyfriend she did some wrist-slitting a few weeks afterwards. It was quite serious because she collapsed and was taken to hospital and she was put in a psychiatric ward and I was told to visit her so I had to take the bus down there to see her.

When I went to college she was working in a bar and at some time she started taking drugs. I think she began taking heroin around 1985 and then she left Washington to go to Australia, I think it was to try again to get off the drugs. She did as much as anyone could have done to stop taking heroin. She died in 1998 in Sydney of an overdose after going through rapid detox. I didn't see her again after she left Washington.

The last time I did see her it was nice. There had been another episode with another boyfriend of mine and we were both still obsessed with the past and we drank and talked a lot and did a lot of frantic dashing around and we got on better because we were in our twenties and both a bit older.

I did hear her voice once; she had come to the US and I had moved into a new apartment and it was a mess and I heard her voice on the answerphone and it was a peculiar feeling.

It was completely different for my older sister. She was seven when our parents did the rearranging and I think that she and her stepsister were more established as little selves. My sister said that when I hadn't seen my dad for those seven years I had felt as if he didn't love me, whereas she had known he loved us. She pretended our father was a nice uncle.

We are very different, my sister and I. I excavate forever and she doesn't and that's what's made her a solid person. My sister was the first person to read my book and she was shocked first of all and said she hadn't realised many of the things I had felt. I think part of the shock was that initially I had used real names and to see all of these things she had blanked out was shocking for her, but she has been very generous about the book. I'm close to her. Because we had those others, we didn't have the struggles that other sisters have between them. Some sisters are riven with problems. She and her counterpart stepsister were not so competitive, they were not so desperate to be in the centre as Jenny and I were.

I was living in Germany with my husband when I heard about Jenny. I had been to the grocery shops and I came home and I saw there had been a message left on the answerphone so I hit the button and it was my stepfather and he said, 'Bad news, Jenny's dead.' Just like in the movies I sat down and I thought 'I'm free,' and my next thought was it's too late for me to say I know what we did to each other and I'm sorry.

I was getting ready to go to the funeral but my father said he would rather I didn't come to the funeral because my stepfather would be there and it wouldn't be fair on the other sister. I helped pay for my sister to go. After the funeral my stepfather went to the phone and called me in Germany and said it's over and the other stepsister heard him calling me and started screaming that even then he was calling me.

It's funny when you write a memoir because you can't properly claim that you know how someone else felt. With Jenny I've so often imagined her as in a mirror, trying so hard to get the love of her own father as I tried to get the love of mine, trying just to be seen and recognised by her own father. When you've grown up feeling so replaceable, it's so easy to feel unrecognised, to feel you don't quite exist.

Lucy never had a sister but did not consciously look for one. This may be, she believes, because her friend Beatrice fulfilled that role:

I have never said to Beatrice that she is like a sister to me although we do say we are like family. She has sisters, so she doesn't need any more, but because she was the youngest by some years she wasn't that close to them. Her family lived next door but one to ours and our mothers were close because they were both at home looking after us. I'm not sure how they got to know each other but I don't have a memory of life before Beatrice. I know our mothers became closer when Beatrice's father died. Beatrice is nearly two years younger than me, which was perfect. I was the first to read and was proficient quite quickly so I would read to Beatrice, loudly to make sure the

adults could see me and go, 'How sweet, Lucy's reading to
Beatrice, isn't she clever.' Beatrice remembers my reading
to her (and I'm not sure I didn't make some of the reading
up as I wasn't that good) as an act of generosity. I was
always round her house, after school, where my mother
would already be sitting at the kitchen table drinking tea, or
at weekends when I was bored at home. Their house was
so close I could just pitch up there.

Beatrice had four older sisters and they seemed incredibly glamorous, probably to both of us. They wore fashionable clothes and talked about grown-up things quietly and
had friends round to listen to music with, not to play making
their dolls fall in love with each other like Beatrice and I

were doing in the sitting room. Their house was much live-
lier than ours because of these sisters and the comings and
goings of their friends and the atmosphere was more
relaxed. No fuss was made when the older girls started
smoking and having boyfriends over. It was an open house;
anyone was welcome.

Of course these older sisters did everything before us,
which I found comforting as you could see life mapped out
and imagine what it might feel like to have a half-naked
young man draped over you, or to sit round a table getting
indignant about a war in a country I'd never heard of.

Their house was also bigger than ours, clean but slightly
shabby (although ours was messier) and they had a big garden with vegetables and fruits that we used to nibble at.

I hardly remember Beatrice at primary school, although
she says I helped her when she was bullied in the playground. This makes me wonder anxiously if I should have
done more. I don't remember her being unhappy as I was
busy fighting for my own friendships. I suspect like real
sisters, I had my year group to play with at school and she
had hers and we waited until we got home to play together.

Beatrice and I went to different secondary schools. Our
'playing' at her house
felt more grown-
up as our lives
separated
and we both
had new
friends. I
was keen on

learning while she struggled more at school; I'm not sure
why as she's intelligent and interested but she may have
lacked confidence. Her older sisters were designated the
smart ones and maybe she felt the brains had run out when
they got to her. But they hadn't. Quite often we would sit in
her bedroom (which would often be changed as various
sisters moved out or moved back) and talk about what her
sisters were up to and who and what we wanted to be when
we were older. We knew each other well, really well, and we
spent hours talking and giggling and confiding in each
other about nothing much, but it felt like important stuff.
We had other best friends but there was no jealousy, I think
we saw our relationship as more than a friendship.

When I went off to university I still saw her at holidays
but she didn't visit me, she was always a homebody. In the
summer I would go round and she would always be in the
garden; her skin would turn a magnificent peachy brown
and I, who would have been cooped up in a library for half
the summer, would feel envious of her colour and her freedom. One day, on hearing from my mother that I was broke
she sent me £50 which was quite a lot of money then, and I
know she didn't have much herself. I've always seen that as
a concerned sisterly thing to do.

We gradually eased apart. My family moved away and
our mothers met less frequently. I doubt that we actively
missed each other, although she was so much a part of my
childhood that few memories didn't include her. I felt, like
family, she would always be accessible if I needed her. I
heard that she had got married (as a child it would have
been inconceivable that I wouldn't have been invited but

the wedding was small and quick) and had children. I no longer had her number but made half-hearted attempts to track her down. As time went on it felt embarrassing to contact her; why now, why hadn't we bothered before?

One day, I was in a corner shop near where my family used to live. We were visiting my mother and the children had been begging for sweets. I heard her voice first: 'Lucy?' Did I know before I turned round? I think so. There was a moment of awkwardness and then it felt normal. We have never gone over the time when we didn't know each other. It was as if we had stepped out of each other's lives only briefly, because we'd been busy. We found we liked each other's partners, children, that we were still the same and the more so whenever we were together. We ring and see each other as much as work and motherhood allows. But she is there again now, she who knew my father better than my partner did, who understands my relationship with my mother, who is on my side. It turns out, she admitted some months later, that she had seen me go into the shop and followed me. I love the fact she did that.

15

How to Be a Good Sister

What does it mean to be a good sister and are you under any obligation to be one? There isn't one blueprint to follow, and by the time you're reading this you will already have your own way of being a sister. You may have a close, mildly friendly or distant relationship. But however things stand, your life will have been shaped by having or being a sister, so a few tips on how to improve on that relationship shouldn't go amiss.

Stephen P. Bank and Michael D. Kahn are American psychologists who say that the bond between siblings is often expressed viscerally and strongly at an unconscious level, without the siblings necessarily understanding the relationship. Rather poetically, they argue in *The Sibling Bond* that there is

> a sixth sense that this relationship is vital to one's knowledge of oneself. One's core self, seen through the eyes of a sibling or compared with that of a sibling, remains as one essential reference point for personal identity. Because no words can ever capture these impressions, sibling conflict at the core remains the most difficult to resolve.

Although being a good sister to a sister has some differences from being a good sister to a brother, there is much overlap. For a sister to say she does not unequivocally love her sister or brother may be difficult because it may feel unnatural. But it's inevitable at times to be irritated by, to envy and to dislike your sibling. Such feelings may be disturbing because they may come out of the blue. To stand a chance of having a healthy relationship Bank and Kahn suggest you do the following:

Be close (but make sure you are your own person)
Be loving (but not too intensely)
Be co-operative
Be loyal
Be admiring
Be tolerant

They also say it's fine to be competitive and even aggressive, although hair-pulling and sly kicking are best not continued into adulthood. Other psychologists advise that siblings should not boast about their achievements (surely not a good thing to do in any relationship) or claim that they are better than their sister at anything, unless it's an obscure activity that no one wants to be any good at – but even that's debatable. It's also a bad idea to compare yourself with your sister, although understandable. Brothers do it as well as sisters, usually around sporting achievements as sisters traditionally do better academically. It's rather illogical to compare yourself to your siblings as there are plenty of other people you could compare yourself with. If your parents have compared the two

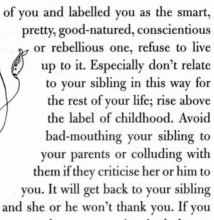

THE MUSICAL ONE

of you and labelled you as the smart, pretty, good-natured, conscientious or rebellious one, refuse to live up to it. Especially don't relate to your sibling in this way for the rest of your life; rise above the label of childhood. Avoid bad-mouthing your sibling to your parents or colluding with them if they criticise her or him to you. It will get back to your sibling and she or he won't thank you. If you are a sister, never borrow your sister's clothes or buy the same ones without asking and never ever make a play for her partner. Both are crimes against the sisterhood. If you are the sister of a brother one of the worst things you can do, apart from telling tales about him, is to be intimidating or mean-spirited to his girlfriend, whenever he should get one. Surveys show that sisters-in-law are often not held in great affection, so try, for your brother's sake, to be the best of breed.

As you get older, don't fight over your childhood memories and who has the accurate version. Siblings have selective memories, sometimes conveniently forgetting the more painful incidents of childhood. There is no need to rub your sister's nose into the memory of her wetting herself in assembly or crying uncontrollably because she lost her comfort blanket. Some sisters find it impossible to stop competing as adults over who has the better career, the more desirable partner and the more talented children. Try to resist this temptation, as there's really no point in it. Comparisons between brothers and sisters are no less odious for being less direct.

Being a sister or having one is a lifelong commitment, so it works best if you can support each other, understanding that like all relationships it is likely to ebb and flow through the cycle of life. As adults you may face the pain of coping with ageing parents and the challenges of bringing up children, working and keeping your own relationships happy. Having a sister to confide in, laugh with, and above all to be on your side against anything that isn't, is invaluable. This doesn't mean you have to be best friends or that you need to feel guilty if you aren't close to your sister. But it does mean you should make your best efforts not to offend each other and at least try to be loyal and trustworthy.

In her book about siblings, *My Dearest Enemy, My Dangerous Friend*, the psychologist Dorothy Rowe says that siblings who have been estranged should consider trying to become reconciled. To do this, she says, you need to be willing to talk about your childhood and your relationship and to be specific about any incidents that have hurt either of you. The reason for doing this is not to pick at old wounds but to accept responsibility for what happened and forgive each other. In some families this is not an easy process, as all families have rules about what can and what cannot be talked about. Similarly the family version of a story is the one that usually prevails. The purpose is not to disrupt the family by chewing over old crimes and concocting your own version of events but to talk, as siblings, about what family events meant to you. Rowe says you shouldn't be resistant to an appraisal of your own childhood.

Even more importantly, Rowe says, don't be resentful or bitter about your sister's life. Any version of 'I could have done as well as her if only . . .' should be stamped on immediately. There is no mileage in either judging your sister or expecting her to think or act as you do. Which after all is the beauty of having a sister.

Acknowledgements

There were many sisters I spoke to in writing this book and I am immensely grateful to all of them for sharing their insights and stories. I would like to thank my brother for his encouragement and for making me a sister in the first place. Thanks especially to the writers who generously wrote their stories for this book; Amy Fleming at the *Guardian*, Alice O'Keefe, at the *Bookseller*, John Holborow and Ann Robinson. Julie Showalter's story was kindly given by her husband Allan Showalter MD. The Jane Austen Society and Ann Dinsadale at the Charlotte Brontë Association were both helpful in providing detailed information that I could never have got from just reading published biographies. I am very grateful to Susan Polgár, an amazing champion of and for chess, for letting me interview her and tell her story, and also to Jane Allison, for letting me do the same. Thanks also to Professor Simon Goldhill for advising me on Greek sisters.

The staff at the British Library were, as anyone who has been there will know, fantastically helpful.

I have enjoyed writing this book not only because sisterhood is such an absorbing subject but because it's both fun and a privilege to work with my editor at Faber, Belinda Matthews. I'm also very grateful for the skills of Kate Ward and Eleanor Rees at Faber and for Stephanie Von Reiswitz's glorious illustrations which would light up any book.

Thanks to people who work in my local bookshop (The Muswell Hill Bookshop) for both suggesting sisters to write about and for putting my books in their window.

Thanks to my family, John, Sam, Maddy, Tilly, Lydia and my mother for putting up with my working on and talking about sisters every evening and weekends for over a year, and to my agent, Rachel Calder at the Sayle Literary Agency, for being supportive and trusting me to get on with it. Also to John's sisters Kate, Helen and Lily for their ideas on which sisters should be included in this book. I'd like to thank Morag, who I met at Villa Pia, for kick-starting my thoughts on sisters by sharing her experiences.

At the time of going to press some permissions have yet to be returned. If these and any I have missed are in copyright or need payment for use, please let either me or Faber know.

Extracts from *Rena's Promise* by Rena Kornreich Gelissen and Heather Dune Macadam, published by Weidenfeld & Nicolson

Extract from *If the Spirit Moves You* by Justine Picardie, published by Picador imprint/ Pan Macmillan (www.panmacmillan.com)

Extract from *Lifetime Guarantee* by Alice Bloch, published by Persephone Press, Inc.

Extracts from *Florence Nightingale* by Cecil Woodham Smith, published by Constable and Company

Extract from *No Bed of Roses* by Joan Fontaine, published by W. H. Allen

Extract from *Blackberry Winter* by Margaret Mead, published by William Morrow Pocket Editions, a division of Simon & Schuster

Extract from 'To Cherish the Life of the World' from *Selected Letters of Margaret Mead*, edited by Margaret M. Caffrey and Patricia A. Francis, published by Basic Books, Perseus Books Group

Extract from *Memoirs of a Dutiful Daughter* by Simone de Beauvoir, translated by James Kirkup (Andre Deutsch and Weidenfeld & Nicolson, 1959, Penguin Books, 1963). Copyright Librairie Gallimard, 1958. This translation copyright The World Publishing Company, 1959

Extracts from letters by the Brontës reprinted from *The Brontës* with permission from the author, Juliet Barker. The book is published by Phoenix, Orion Books Ltd

Extract from *Selected letters of Vanessa Bell*, published by Bloomsbury Publishing Ltd

Virginia Woolf's suicide letter to Vanessa is taken from *The Letters of Virginia Woolf*, published by Hogarth Press. Reprinted by permission of Random House Group Ltd.

Letter from Christabel to Sylvia Pankhurst is reprinted with permission from Richard Pankhurst. It is taken from *Women's History* review Volume 10, Number 3, 2001